TALENT
ALL IN ALL

Dr. Dragan P. Bogunovic MD

authorHOUSE®

AuthorHouse™
1663 Liberty Drive
Bloomington, IN 47403
www.authorhouse.com
Phone: 1 (800) 839-8640

Published by AuthorHouse   06/29/2015

ISBN: 978-1-5049-1255-6 (sc)
ISBN: 978-1-5049-1254-9 (e)

Print information available on the last page.

Any people depicted in stock imagery provided by Thinkstock are models, and such images are being used for illustrative purposes only. Certain stock imagery © Thinkstock.

This book is printed on acid-free paper.

Purpose of writing this book.

On first place it was idea to publicize power of human's talent that is possession of every living humans being.

Even that is possession of everyone born upon this planet earth not everyone has that privilege to enjoy that precious free given gift

My original idea has been expressed in the Title of the book which is: "Talent All in All" which is for all those that are believer founded on Biblical teaching from the book from I Corinthians Ch. 12:4, 5, 6, stating that one Spirit and many gifts. Which means that Talent is Spiritual gift and everyone that acts according to given Gift is never alone, where God is present with that one All in All.

However for those that are not believers Talent means that is All that one soul needs to be successful for the goddesses for all, which is on first place purpose of every Talent. All hard works for All. Whoever you are and whatever your believe is you must believe in the power of Humans talent which is beneficial for All.

ON FIRST PLACE TALENT BELONGS TO EVERYONE THAT IS BORN UPON THIS PLANET EARTH. WHO EVER DISCOVER ITS GIVEN FREE GIFT TALENT, IS NEVER ALONE BUT IS GUIDED AND SUPPORTED BY ALL AND ALL ACCORDING TO LAW OF NATURE WE ALL LIVE UNDER, BECAUSE NATURE IS THE MASTER OVER EVERY TALENT AND EVERY TALENT IS FOLLOWING NATURAL LAW, ONE THAT NEVER EVER DISCRIMINATE AGAINST NO ONE BECAUSE WE ALL BELONG TO NATURE WE LIVE IN.

Once when you develop your given gift to the maximal level you are in the rank of Genius, which in this moment you are not in submission of nature but master of the nature.

Talent is free gift but hard work made it Genius. Nature is master over every talent while Genius is master over the nature.

In my life my one small talent was never alone without protection and support to in every occasion presents when ever is needed.

1

We may then concluded that Talent is everything in every moment of our lives.

. It is also firmly stated that every talent needs humans abilities in order to act with good results. It requires persistence's, perseverance's, endurances, strength, motivation, curiosity, attentiveness to never give up, will power and many others different believes.

However some believe that talent is not only skill that needs many different abilities but that many mention things above could be present in different people as Talent. For example Albert Einstein stated that he has no talent but his power his curiosity we may call his talent

There are so many different people living upon this planet earth with each one blessed with different talent or talents.

As many different people are so many different talents are to fit for every person at the time. Everyone is authentic so every talent is also authentic for that person.

As it was stated in beginning of the book that we all possess talents and also our power for talent to work is in our ability or abilities working together in consortium for better performance.

We also stated according to our evolve knowledge that one is talent and that talent may not only be skill but also so many different things that we previously described as abilities.

That all must be something new knowledge that is here placed for further debate.

With many of this powerful wise sentences I intend to present to every family every education and every society necessity for proper treatment of every new born child that is born with powerful talent, that is born as artist in order to preserve those inborn qualities.

My personal one talent I would call motivation to made me become medical Doctor with talent to be happy and satisfied in my life who I am and what I have as it is also stated by Woody Allan.

I also believe in me as one who works 110% (another talent of my) as per Alfred Adler. Talent is also being busy all the time. Being confident in self and working hard which is as we stated many time for life of every talent. Also discipline is one of most powerful talent on a way to successful life.

However there is no end in describing all those talents that are existing in our world.

Talent is what you are. what you do and what you like to do. Working your Talent is on first place satisfaction happiness and joy. In one word Talent is FUN

Purpose of my book and especially last five chapters-Practice to incite readers to come to their own conclusion as I did and for us as a part of our Humanity to create common program for the benefits for eentire humanity

For the same reason I also add 5 chapters of practice with those aphorisms and challenging questions to incite readers to think and to meditated about importance of humans talent for the future of their children, society and entire humanity.

However everyone is directed in real life by its own experiences what is my initial idea and purpose to see if anyone has same or different experience from my own experience. It will be of interest for me to see is some of the readers will come with same conclusion as I have in 50 years as practical medical physician and later in writing my books mainly about humans free gift talent which I firmly believe that Talent which is born and educated well is everything that one needs because talent is not only skill but everything that I did present as humans abilities.

Talent is greatest power of love as power of humans skill for certain activities that also encompass all those human's abilities as endurance, perseverance, persistence's and many others because as my title states that talent is all in all because when I do follow my given free gift my talent I am never alone because One who is giver of my gift is always with me as my supporter my endurance my encouragement that I am not acting alone but I am team with One Greatest Power for all believers or not.

As I see myself as a part of humanity that was created based on certain principles and certain purpose for the better life for entire creation and everything directed and empowered with that free gift which is for me human's talent as a savior of the entire world.

In one word What present human's talent is: every human's life PURPOSE.

Last 5 chapters that I call practice is given with certain purpose as I already mentioned to read to meditated and to become more familiar with what is important, which is given power for the better life for their children and also to respond to my challenging questions in order for all together to create the best way for proper education of every born child.

I hope that they will be able to become partaker to spread in positive way idea about importance of humans Talent for every living soul and entire humanity, as active protégée.

I will be eternally grateful to all those who read this book and present their opinion about so important question to enlarge or understanding for betterment of entire humanity..

Dr Dragan P. Bogunovic MD

Introduction #1

"Every child comes with a message that God is not yet discourage of man."
Rabindranath Tagore

Everyone arrives to this world with talent and no one is excluded. Talent comes as a free gift but is not free from responsibilities. Talent encompasses everybody's life, purpose and direction.

"A life without purpose is directionless. Without purpose, one gets pulled by every passing pleasure and pushed by every fear." Jonathan Lockwood Huie.

Talent is our life's purpose.

I present to you the case of Dr. J., a practicing Orthopedic surgeon. His unsuccessful career hit the wall when many hospitals closed the door to his practice. A close friend of his, also an Orthopedic surgeon, recommended including arthroscopy as a testing procedure. Through hard work, research and dedication, Dr. J continued his career as a successful Orthopedic surgeon, specializing in arthroscopy. His talent and passion encouraged him to write a successful book on arthroscopy. Although he discovered his talent later in life, he used his given gift, his talent, to finish its medical career as successful orthopedic surgeon in arthroscopy.

This is a true story that show the power of human talent. Talent is never old and never late.

Talent is the free gift grunted to every living soul as a given free but not free from great responsibilities. Talent is exhibited in the form of love. It resides in every humans' heart and contains our life's purpose. It leads us in the right direction so long as we believe in its power and love.

Talent is spiritual gift with one Spirit but many different gifts. It is given to each of us, from God, according to our personal abilities working All in All. It is certainly a Spiritual gift that no one living soul has ever physically seen but can be observed as the fruits or outcome of that precious and powerful gift.

While Talent is Spiritual power, the ability to act out of our talent is our fleshly power that is used as the foundation for talent. Successful talent fits to its abilities much like a key in a lock. Enduring hard work supports our talent which fits into life's big picture. Opening the door of opportunity can be seen as the reward we are given for using our God given talent.

There are many definitions of human talent and most of them are in agreement that talent is a spiritual power. Most of those definitions also support the idea that talent includes characteristics such as: endurance, perseverance, courage, motivation, will power and many other well known attributes. These characteristics are all supported throughout this book.

This book uses concise phrased statements of both truth and opinion in combination with ancient pieces of popular wisdom. We used only those that are related to human talent and abilities in order to present a clear and true picture of every talented soul and its life.

Many of these traditional and ancient philosophies are repeated purposely in order to make an impression by stressing the importance of human talent for every living soul. Talent has the ability to leave a foot print on the lives of our families, society and humanity as a whole. This imprint is promoted by all those wise and talented people whose names continue to live as a positive boost for the productive of our humanity.

We are conscious that there are many they do not agree with our definition of human talent. We must respect this without any argumentation.

Using our given talent and power accurately undoubtedly has a powerfully influence on living a productive life.

What we should know is that the truth about talent is that it is ours. It serves as directions to life that all can benefit from. It is the truth that no one is excluded from the benefits of talent.

Talent is warm and pleasant much like the electrical power of the sun's rays. In the words of Maya Angelou, "We know that talent is like electricity. We do not understand electricity but we do use it; that all is good that must be used for the goodness for all."

For many years, my talent directed me in the right direction by opening doors of opportunities for my path's way. It was through the power of love that my talent became the strength to open those challenging doors. With courage, I will continue to use my talent through to the end of my path.

Looking back, I may say truthfully that through the power of love, my given talent was my guide to open doors of opportunities and in some time to close those that led to failure. That was the power of my love, my given gift, my talent as my entire life supporter which will last to the last bit of its power.

It is also true that that same power of love, that free gift called talent entered into four of my grandchildren. The first was born with talent to become medical doctor. She graduated medical school and became an Orthopedic surgeon. My second grandchild was born to be an artist. She graduate high school as a national honors student in art. She went on to graduate art school and obtained a masters degree. She is now the CEO of her own company. And my third, who from an early age showed a special love for animals, went on to graduate Veterinary School to become doctor of Veterinary medicine. And my last grandchild decided, according to her heart, to become medical Nurse, being on a way to realize her given gift.

Through my grandchildren, I am confident that my writing will help many other parents, educators and our society to help every newcomer to open their heart and to discover what that one is born "to be." Through adequate education, "to become" as a honorable member of our society for the goodness for all.

To all new parents. To all educators and to all members of our society I do devote this book with the best intention for all, because TALENT is a privilege of every new born upon this planet earth here and no one is ever excused for any reason.

To finish this introduction, I will add a few wise words from well known wise people from the past and some from the present.

"Believe in yourself, and the rest will fall into place. Have a faith in your own abilities, work hard, and there is nothing you cannot accomplish." Brad Henry

"If you have found your truth within yourself there is nothing more in this whole existence to find." Osho

This is all about your talent. You have to discover what is going to be your life existence, your success and your happiness.

"Refuse to be average. Let your heart soar as high as it will." Alden Wilson Tozer

"Open your heart and let your talent free to soar as high as its given power"-Dragan P. Bogunovic.

Family #2

"Every Talent is born in family. Dressed in education. Indoctrinated in society, and rewarded in Universe." Dragan

"Love begins at home, and it is not how much we do, but how much love we put in that action." Mother Teresa

Every talent is born in family, because family provides not only love but loving care, peace, security and encouragement, for every child to decide by itself according to his heart.

Every child will discover their free gift in its heart as soon as child is able to behold in this world what is written in its heart. Love instantly comes out to become married for its future occupation for life. That is what happens to every child but differs depending on how each one responds.

Not every child responds in same way. Some accept their given gift to become part of their future life and some not. Those that discover that precious gift begin to slowly express their hearts desire as love for their given gift and become supported and encouraged by their parents.

For those that missed their gift, their next chance is offered through the educational system. They provide the opportunity for that child to open their heart and to continue to search for their gift.

One of first signs that a child has opened his heart and discover his given gift is by showing an interest and love for some activity/s that are in close relation with his gift.

"If you love what you do and feel, that is matter." Katherine Graham

If you love what you do you must be certain that this is your talent. What you are and what you love is your talent.

It is important at an early age for parents to look and carefully observe all those positive signs without any intervention. It is a natural yet slowly occurring processes that needs constant encouragement and support.

It is same process as natural childbirth where a doctor and midwife do not do anything but observe assuring that the natural process is void of life threatening errors.

They must always look for signs of heart as a sign of love, which is inborn power of love from given talent which is itself power of love. Every young one will act from its heart as a sign of love as a sign of pleasure which is acting talent from that youngster heart.

It is so important that entire process starts as earlier as possible. Parents must always remember that birth of every talent is natural like every birth in this world.

New born talent is similar to a newborn child. It requires special loving care and needs to observed to ensure proper development. It's development requires loving care, without any pressure. It must grow naturally in order to mature, like everything else in life.

"You are a child of God. Your playing small does not serve the world. There is nothing enlightening about shrinking so that other people won't feel insecure about you. We were born to manifest the glory of God that is within us." *Marianne Williamson.*

What is within us is our given gift, our precious talent, our future life and our future life happiness.

Every parents primary goal is the future of their progeny and especially their given gift which will give them direction in life.

I recommend that mothers or fathers keep a diary of their child and/ or children's activities. That record must be kept diligently and then introduced to the child when he or she enters the educational system.

It is important for parent's to introduces this diary to their child's teachers and to talk about their child's passions. This conversation will stress the importance of their given gift as something that should always keep in their heart as a personal compass that will help guide them through life.

"What you are is God's gift to you. What you become is your gift to God." Anthony Dalla Willa

Your given grace and talents are the most precious gifts to be kept as a life treasure, throughout your entire life.

"God depend on us. It is through us that God is achieved." Andre Gid.

God works through our given talent, All in All, in order to accomplish its predicted planed purpose for us.

Those that believe that we were all born with a talent must pass this wisdom on to their children and more importantly, help them comprehend the importance of finding their talent. They must also understand that gift is free but comes with responsibilities. Similar to electricity, we do not physically see talent but know it is there because of the fruits it offers us.

We do not see spiritual powers like talent just as we do not see electricity however, what we do see is a direct result of its activity.

Talent can be seen as electric power or like a battery. Both exist but have a limited life; without them, we are left in darkness.

"When I stand before God at the end of my life, I would hope that I would not have a single bit of talent left, and could say: I used everything you have give me." Emma Bombeck

Talent is a Spiritual concept as well as a spiritual gift. It must be taken seriously and used as a compass that gives us direction thus, allowing us to understand our purpose in life. You must trust its direction and purpose in order to reach your goals in life.

"Let's start with recognizing your talent and finding ways to serve others by using them." Thomas Kinkaid

No one should be mislead that living a life with talent will be easy because talent comes with practice and hard work. It is an active process. W are connected with power of human's talent for the main purpose to serve each other. That all create one organized society where everyone keep its own position as a life that presents unity.

"Hard work pays off-hard work beats talent any day, but if you are talented and work hard it is hard to beat." Robert Griffin III

We must all understand that Talent is hard work what requires from every member of our society to its best.

This quote from Robert Griffin II should be told to every child prior to them entering our educational system.

We must use this part to speak about Talent, Family, and especially about mother function in family.

"God could not be everywhere, so He created mothers." Jewish proverb

Mother who have endured natural childbirth know firsthand about hard work, dedication, endurance and talent. Similar to childbirth, everything goes slowly and naturally where only patience is right way providing security and success. However, forcing things in life is not natural way that may lead you in the wrong direction as well as complicate things. The endurance and talent of mothers in labor results in one or more human souls being delivered into this world.

The birth of a child is also the birth of new unique human talent. Every *truly* good deed is accompanied by great happiness.

There are two great miracles that exist in our world. The first miracle is the miracle of a child's birth and the second is the birth of human talent.

Mothers hold much of the power of the future of their children because mothers possess unconditional love to endow upon her child's soul. Every mother plays a part in the future of her child.

"We are all born with purpose according to our given gift our talent and we are all entrusted to be able to do that, and to do it well, according to our abilities. Dragan P. Bogunovic

A loving family is similar to a delivery room; a place where new life is born and nurtured.

"Where love is, there is also God" Mohandas (Mahatma) Gandhi

For this reason, every mother should keep diary detailing their child's behavior and activities. This information can be shared with the child's teacher and then utilized in the classroom. Now, the teacher will know that child's strengths and weaknesses and be able to help the child grow.

"All children are born artists. The problem is how to remain an artist once when grow up." Pablo Picasso

Every child is born with power of discovery starting from the first day of its life. They possess the imaginative power to act, to create all according to their age. Eventually that power of discovery will discover what is in their heart, their talent. They only need to be encouraged to do what is in their heart and to never give up doing what they love.

It would be also beneficial for those children to show some interest for some activities to be pared together with other talents, in order to learn that no talent works as a individual but in many cases being even they are different becoming complementary to each other to learn way of united work.

It is well known and accepted that all those different talents work together in unity being complementary to each others for the benefit for successful life for all.

We may also use big hospitals where many different talents work all together in unity being complimentary to each others as one organized orchestra. For one and only one reason to save our lives and make us living better.

That is one the best example that we may observe that no talent can and will not do separate from other talents.

We may conclude that mothers are of utmost importance to our children. Now, we must ourselves ask why so many children that are born in loving families never open their heart to discover their talent.

Every mother is a loving mother but not all mothers have had the opportunity to learn the importance of educating their children on finding their passion in life.

Every future mother must be well informed and educated about that so important role that she will have for the future of their children.

God could not be everywhere, so He created mother." Jewish proverb.

Most important job of mothers is to allow their children to observe and live life so they can find their passion, their gift which will lead them to complete happiness.

It is only when we open our hearts and let power of love our talent come out, that we become married to our talent and our future life. For every family that produces talented children also produces the opportunity for their children to live purposeful lives that will benefit and serve many. We must always be grateful for the given gift that will benefit the lives of our children.

"An ounce of mother is worth a pound of clergy." Spanish proverb.

Thus, it has been written that behind every child's success stands a mother.

Mother's house is house of love where all things take place in natural order.

Everything takes place in a natural way when there is love. Some call this phenomenon a miracle. Love is the house of peace.

"One of the greatest gifts a parents can give a children is to help them find their talent." Sean Lovey.

This is true because every talent is created within a loving family where there is great love and also great understanding about the importance of human talent.

Today we have many different opinions about the origin of human talent.

1. Talent is God's gift.

2. "Being passionate and curious is my talent. I have no special talent. I am only passionate and curious." A. Einstein

3. Intense desire is my talent. "It sometimes seems that intense desire creates not only its own opportunity but its own talent." Eric Holder

4. Some believe that is all in humans genes. "Talent is an accident of genes and responsibility." Alan Rickman

5. Some believe that talent is in the humans brain, in nerve connections called synapses. "Talent is the human filter to accurately filer every situation." Marcus Buckingham (Dr. Harry Chugani)

There are many different beliefs and understandings of talent. We must consider all beliefs and follow what we believe to be true in our hearts. However one thing is true that no one can teach talent.

Here we must state one fact that talent is a privilege given to every living soul. Talent belongs and is given without consideration of skin color, language, nationality religion, political, ideology or even sexual orientation. Believers or not, we must find and use our talent because it is given to everyone to use for both personal and common benefit.

Talent is universal because talent belongs to every living human's soul.

I am certain that our God will not be concerned about whether or not we are believers but am certain that he is concerned about whether or not we take and use the gifts we were given.

If I should argue about that statement I will certainly call your attention to a story about an old man and his two sons. The older son was good and obedient while the younger son was not. The old man asked his older obedient son to try and find a passion in life in order to find security and happiness. The older son agreed yet did not follow through. The younger son stated that he had no interest in finding his path but later in life, through the guidance of his father, took it upon himself to better his life and find his talent.

Everyone has a gift and it is important to utilize this gift as thanks to the higher power that has generously blessed us with it.

Similarly, every mother should be able to instruct older children that they should never aspire to be more than what is given to them. We must act according to the power of our given gifts and never stride to be less of what is given but to stand in position according to its given power.

To achieve less than what has been given to you is a disgrace. Going above what is given to you is disrespectful.

Be who you are and do not go beyond of what is given to you.

"The greatest evil which fortune can inflict on men is to endow them with small talent and great ambition." Luc de Clapier

We must acknowledge that we are all gifted in different ways, no one is excluded. Our purpose in life is to be a productive member of society and help one another.

Everyone is given precious gift and every human soul has same right for education and development in order to live a happy productive life doing what they love.

It is also important for those that are growing to develop healthy relationships with others. Opportunities for success and happiness are endless when we combine different talents.

We must understand that that no one talent should act alone. It should be incorporated with other different talents which will create one powerful unity of one healthy body.

"You don't get harmony when everybody sings same song." Doug Floyd

Parents and mature children should understand that we have only one life and only one talent and only one chance to a have prosperous productive and happy life.

Part B chapter #1 Family.

#1. We must acknowledge that mothers and fathers pave the path our children take. Discovering talent starts with support from home.

#2 Talent is a precious gift that needs to be protected and kept safe from any negative outside influence that may have an obstructive effect, delaying our progress.

#3. Talent is our life and our life purpose. Our talent allows us to conquer anything and also gives us the opportunity to conform to our ever changing world. Talent is our guide and our direction.

#4 What is within us is our given gift, our precious gift, our talent. Our talent allows us to conquer anything and also gives us the opportunity to conform to our ever changing world.

"Listen to the compass of your heart. All you need lives within your." Mary Anne Radmacher

#5 Children must continue to explore different paths until they find the one that leads them to their passion, their talent.

"Through our given talent God works All in All in order to accomplish its predicted planed purpose for you. Dragan.

#6. The purpose of your given talent is to do good for yourself and for others.

"Let start with recognizing your talent and finding ways to serve others by using them." Thomas Kinkaid

#7. No one should be mislead in thinking that living a life with talent means living a happy prosperous life. Talent is of no use without hard work, dedication and commitment.

"Hard work pays off--hard work beats talent any day, but if you are talented and work hard it is hard to be beat." Robert Griffin III

#8. Every child needs to know love and experience love. More importantly, they must be surrounded by it.

#9. Every parent, especially mothers, need to truly understand the importance of talent and its influence on our children's future. We must help our children look for their talent and seize it when found.

#10. Everyone has their own unique talent. Everyone needs the opportunity to discover their talent and this opportunity comes through family, education, and knowledge.

"Everyone has their own talent. It is up to the individual to see what you can actually do." Win Butler

#11. We must know and inform our children when they are ready to enter into the education system, that talent is a free gift that comes with responsibility. Studying and hard work is critical in order for the seed of talent to mature.

"A person has the right, and I think responsibility, to develop all their talents." Josie Norman

#12. It is given to be used and not to be wasted.

"We cannot take any credit for our talents. It is how we use them that counts." Madeleine Leang

#13. We must eventually come to some conclusion that our families, our education system and our society needs some education about the importance of human talent for the life for entire humanity and not only family education and society.

#14. Talent is a free gift but not free from responsibilities.

Smith presses the idea that being selfless is in our nature. Although we have been conditioned to think about ourselves first, we must think about others, specifically our family, and do what is necessary to guide them. Mothers and fathers alike, are constantly watching over their children and should do their best to guide them into doing what is right.

Talent is your love and if you miss your talent you miss your life.

Education #3

Education is not preparation for life; education is life." John Dewey. It is all about life, for every member of coming generations to be well prepared according to each one needs. *"It is with children that we have the best chance of studying the development of logical knowledge, mathematical knowledge, physical knowledge, and so forth." Jean Plaget"*

We teach general education with great attention towards individual needs and abilities. Children are all talented and we must educate them and prepare them for their future.

"We should seek system that provides outlets for those skills

and talents so that everyone can find a way to work and serve

in a manner that best suits the strength of each individual."

Lee R. Raymond

It must be requirement that every new student enter our educational system with a written record of their personal talent and abilities. In our system education is programmed for general knowledge and not for what that one is expecting to do in his active life. We must have a both.

The direction is which education starts a man will determined

his future life." Plato.

Proper education starts with typical academia but must also include programs that are directed to educating every child's talent. This is nothing new and is a idea that has been practiced for centuries.

"If I were again beginning my studies, I would follow the advice

of Plato and start with mathematics," Galileo Galilei.

Galileo learned later in life that proper education in his early life, would help him later become a better man; a talented man of production whose work would benefit all of society. Not only Galileo but also many before him and also after him did miss al lot being not treated according to their needs, according to their given talent as a life purpose. for the betterment for entire humanity. I have no doubt that our educational programs have the ability to accommodate all those that are already dedicated to their future life. Positive action will do many goods for family, society and all of humanity. As I think back to my years of medical school, I recall joining programs and classes that did not have medical curriculum. I personal join sports medicine group "kruzok" meaning group of students interested in sports medicine program

"The whole purpose of education is to turn mirror into window."

Sydney J. Harris

Everyone that is born with their own mirror that needs attention in order to be turned into a window. Talent is a mirror that needs proper education in order to become window that opens the view to entire world.

"Better keep yourself clean and bright; you are the window through which you must see the world." George Bernard Shaw.

Keep your talent clean, as it is your window to see the life in front of you. It is all in the hands of our educational systems to do what they are made to do. This means focusing on general education but also preparing every single human soul for its future life.

"Educating the mind without educating the heart is no education at all." Aristotle

Yes, education is the catalyst that will hone and sharpen our

talent, skill and cause them to blossom.

Joseph B. Wirthin

We should have a plethora of well informed professors that work one on one with both students and parents. It is important to consider the needs of students' on an individual basis. Some students enter school with a plan for their future while others do not. We must treat them equally and make their success our number our priority. In that case close cooperation is of utmost importance.

There are different types of talents and intelligences, and

traditional schools sometimes ignore the creative ones.

"It is important for us to give kids every platform for them to

find what they are good at and what they love.

The arts also provide a space for newfound creativity."

Caity Lotz

This important statement must be repeated many times not only in schools but also in the homes of children. It speaks about what they are good at and what they love: That is the clear picture of what in their children heart is; to direct that kind of almost that we may say spiritual action.

"To me, education is leading out of what is already there, in the pupils soul."

Heath L. Buckmaster.

That is a clear presentation of their heart and expression of love from their heart which is their desire of every talented one. Talent is the power of love from their heart, their talents to be educated in same way as we educate mind of our children.

And their reaction to this world comes through love, in the form of a skill. Love what you do, and do what you love. A mother's delivery is a slow and difficult process that should not last over 24 hrs. It is endured and accomplish with some pain and endurance which leads to endless joy and happiness.

In the child's case, it may take not in hours but rather years of endurance and persistence to deliver newborn-talent for their prosperous and happy future life. We must be patient as it takes time to enter into the next step in program which is customized according to their given new born talent.

Lily Bogunovic- First year resident in orthopedics surgery Washington University St Louis explains how she discovered her passion for medicine: "I knew I wanted to be a physician since fifth grade." Dr Lily Bogunovic is passionate about her chosen profession. Dr Bogunovic recalls working in her grandfather's medical clinic throughout high school and college breaks: "He was a gynecologist in Yugoslavia before moving to Wisconsin and opening up a family practice. I accompanied my grandfather to early morning rounds at various Milwaukee hospitals. It was though shadowing him that I knew I wanted to be a medical doctor.'" -Lily Bogunovic, MD left her rural roots and went on to graduate from Cornell University and ten Weill Cornell Medical College in New York. As she debated a medical specialty she blended her interest in surgery with a love of sports and the outdoors. She lives her life supported by a loving and carrying family. Her family lives on a farm close to nature. It takes patience to realize that when you plant the seed, you must work hard before you receive fruits or your reward. It is true because nature is master over the tlent and every act of talented one is act according to natural law. *Nature does not hurry, yet everything is accomplished"* Lao Tzu Living life in accordance to nature made allowed her to open her heart. Her two sisters and one brother did the same. Being close to the nature creates nothing but magic and personal power to open your heart. In time, the power of your given talent will become free and show you the directions to happiness." *Artistic talent is a gift from God and whoever discovers it in himself have an obligation to know that he cannot waste this talent, but must develop."*

Pope John Paul II

Every talent must be discovered prior to entering into the educational system. Education gives us the tools we need in order to master our talents so we can live a prosperous and meaningful life." Education is equally as important as talent. Talent is life and can be viewed as a key that opens the doors to success and happiness.

"Education is the most powerful weapon which you can use to change the world"

Nelson Mandela.

Every educated talent while moving through its life gaining necessary experience and also move forward our humanity toward better life for all.

Education is important however, we must not neglect the future life of that student. We must ask what that student loves and how that love can guide them into creating a future. A life void of talent is a life void of direction. Talent is life's purpose.

I believe that poor performance in school is a direct result of a lack of guidance and direction. Without guidance and direction, students have no desire to do well. They lack the inspiration to grow and mature which leaves them directionless. However, educators must for those children, present new fertile ground to plant their newly discovered seeds. Encourage students to find their talent so they can flourish and thrive.

"Much education is monumentally ineffective. All too often we

are giving young *people cut flowers when we should be*

teaching them to grow their own plants."

John W. Gardner

Talent is the seed that must be planted in educational fields in order to grow into mature plants which may bear fruits for all to thrive. It is said that talent is born in families but dressed in education. Programs must be introduced in every school as a part of every child's education so we know that our children are entering life with the tools they need in order to succeed.

"Every education without Talent is lame and every Talent

without education is *blind." DraganP. Bogunovic- MD*

We must publicize talent in all of our educational programs and know that it is through education that we mastery our talent. The second part of this book is up for your personal interpretation. It stress the importance of talent and its impact on our current and future generation. All together we will be able to invent the best educational programs for all of our children with a goal of maximizing their potential to impact the world in which we live. I will leave you to consider this thought from Ashfag Ishaq: *"We humans have not yet achieved our full creative potential primarily because every child's creativity is not properly nurtured. The critical role of imagination, discovery and creativity in child's education in only beginning to come to light and, even with the education community, many still do not appreciate or realize its vital importance."* Ashfag Ishaq Every child is born with the power of discovery. This power is present from the first day of their life and is utilized while observing and perceiving all things presented to them. Every child is also born with power of imagination. When these powers are combined, we can say that every child is an artist. The issue is how to preserve the artist in each child. How do we keep the flame from burning out? We must be certain to protect all of the gifts that each child enters this world with. By protecting these gifts, we are promoting these gifts. Protecting their gifts is also protecting and securing their future. Only when they are ready, can these gifts be opened. *"Seeds of great discovery are constantly floating around us, but they only take root in minds well prepared to receive them."* Joseph Henry The doors of opportunities are wide open in our living nature for all that are well prepard in education syste according to their given talent their given life purpose for better life for entire humanity.

We must take human's talent seriously and give every child opportunity to advance in his or hers given natural ower. It is future life of our children and future life of our entire humanity.

Society #4

"If people knew how hard I worked to get my mastery, it would not seem so wonderful at all"- *Michelangelo*. That is the future for all talented people entering society, entering real life. Society has the large responsibility of providing the right vocational place for those that are well prepared for a life of hard work and endurance. There are situations when students go from family, through the educational system, without opening their heart and discovering their precious gift their Talent, to become their life direction for their educated soul. However, we must expect the arrival of those that did not accomplish their initial responsibility, the responsibility to open their heart and find out who they are born to be lies on every society to do it in time necessary for complete recovery of the talented soul. For that reason every society must be well prepared for that occasion because every lost talent is loss for every society and even for entire humanity because you will never know what that lost talent is born to do for the goodness for all.

They must open their hearts prior to entering our education system in order to become one according to its given gift. Yes, talent is the gift. As we mentioned before, everyone has to have some degree of education and possess a given Talent-their life purpose, in order to become a complete person able to succeed in society. Our society has to take on the role of family particularly the role of a mother. We must utilize the power of education in order to help everyone entering into this active life. We are incomplete without our given life power, our life direction and purpose given to us through our readymade Talent. If we may believe our talents our life commitments are also our salvation as long as we do hard work according to our given gift our talent. *"I am a poor man and of little worth who is laboring-hard work-in that art that God has given me in order to extend my life as long as possible. Michelangelo Buonarotti*. Talent is the gift given with certain purpose. Talent is also hard work for every talented one. Talent is also great responsibility and in same time according to Michelangelo way to extend your life upon this planet earth until you accomplish your given duty. That all is also closely related to each other creating one grand life purpose for every living and acting soul. There are many reasons for failure however, the most prominent being poor financial support. Poverty and lack of education are two of the most common reasons children fail to open their gift. This also leads to poor results throughout their education. It is well known fact that children without the ambition to find their passion (talent) perform purely in school because there is no incentive to do well and no future plans involving their talent. Proper care of these children starts in our school system. Education allows children to eventually become active contributing members of society.

All children that perform poorly in school must be evaluated. There is always a reason for poor performance but most importantly is to find a solution. Evaluations must be performed in order to provide adequate care and to continue proper education with an emphasis on the future life (talent) of every child. *"The sign of a good society is where talent is respected."* *Irrfan Khan* Our children are our future, not only the future of our nation but the future of our entire humanity. The entire world must recognize that every child represents our future and that one child is equally as important as the other. *"We must not lose faith in our humanity."* Gandhi. We are humanity and humanity is our lives.

An educated and benevolent society is one not only with a brain but also with a heart able to resemble the function of a mother. This society contains an educational system with the power and ability to accomplish what should have been done a long time ago. However, that kind of action is never late because that action is one that brings to our life, to our society, and even to entire humanity, hope for a better life for us all. Talent is free gift and great responsibility with a place in every society. Society has the great responsibility of assuring that every child has its own vocational working place for the benefit for all.*" Whenever a youth is ascertained to possess talents meriting an education which parents cannot afford, he should be carried forward at the public expense."James Madison*. We must all agree that this action is not only a moral responsibility but for every human society a spiritual obligation; *"Artistic talents are a gift from God and whoever discovers it in himself has a certain obligation: to know that he cannot waste this talent, but must develop it." Pope John Paul II*. Talent is free gift given with certain purposes related to the power of that given gift. *"It is spiritual given gift-your talent - that must not go in vain but to develop through education and used for beneficial purpose for all." Dragan P. Bogunovic, MD.* In such a situation, society becomes an open door of opportunity for all those that arrive without being properly equipped for a successful life supported by all. Society takes on the role of family, educational system, a corporation, religious society and many other responsible parts of our society." *There can be no keener revelation of a society's soul than the way in which it treats its children"*

Nelson Mandela

It is the responsibility of society to help children who, through the negligence of family and education, have been left alone without their given power. That child's success and future is now in the hands of society, for it is the ethical duty of society to help these children. In such a situation, society and our school systems must work together as a family, with the common purpose of saving these neglected children and their given talents. The entire life of every society depends upon its new generation of young and perspective members and their readiness to accept and do their given duty according to their given power their Talent. Those that were treated well will one day become our representative and will certainly remember all those good things that society did for them and will do for generations to come. In order for everything to work properly, there must be a close relation between Family and our education system with family on one side and society on other. When every young man enters life in its society must have some record to carry with about his talent from family and education to present for society to follow up and no one to be lost. Society must be also well informed about importance that every talent finds its proper working place which is in relation to his ability and given power what talent is. It is important that every child has a record containing insight from their mother and/or father about that child's passions as well as a detailed record from teachers or professors highlighting that child's skills and abilities. Our talents our skills mature through experience so, it is important to have a written record from every child's teacher stating their thoughts on what can and should be done to obtain optimal growth for this child and their talents. Those that enter society with these records are guaranteed a place and position in society. They are guaranteed the opportunity to continue working on and perfecting their skill which will in some way benefit the lives of all.

Our society has the ever important responsibility of recognizing upcoming talents and to gives these talented individuals the necessary tools to advance and master their talent. Combining different unique talents is done with team work which then creates one powerful working unit.

"So powerful is the light of unity that it can illuminate the whole world."
Baha'u'llah.

When united, talented people everywhere will bring light-prosperity to the whole world. Unity is power. However, for those that come without a record, society has an obligation to help each child discover what they were destined to be. It is through our talent that we contribute to society and become a worthy member of our progressive society. That is their last chance and society must do their utmost to discover and to educate those who are struggling, for the sake of their lives and for the future of our society.

"Any human anywhere will blossom in a hundred unexpected Talents and capacity simple being given the opportunity to do so." Doris Lessing

Yes, they will need your help and for you to provided an opportunity to wake that sleepy giant that power human talent.

"Vocational education program have made a real difference in the lives of countless young people nationwide; they build self-confidence and leadership skills by allowing students to utilize their unique gifts and Talents." Conrad Burns

This is the right way and the only opportunity for those whose family and educators missed their opportunity. In this case, society took on the role of a "mother" and educational system, in order to provide a good and prosperous life for those that were unfortunate and on their way to losing what has been predestined for them and for society. For some reason their opportunity was lost in time. For the sake of everyone in society and in our nation, we must convene and make recommendations as to what these individuals can do in order to locate their talent and make up for time lost.

"Whenever a youth is ascertained to possess talents meriting an education which his parents cannot afford, he should be carried forward at the public expense." James Madison

This issue does not pertain to our education system alone but also to our society. We must, as a society, cooperate, unite and provide proper education for those that are in need due to financial difficulties. Again and again we cannot more to emphasize importance of good coordination between family education and society.

"I hope that we can continue this cooperation on other critical issues related to America's future technological competitiveness. We must work together to encourage the creative talents that have made our country the world elder in technology." Dan Lipinski.

Similar to the human body, our Talents increase and become stronger through use. Talent that is notused will atrophy much like a muscle that is not being used. It is not solely societies responsibility but also up to family and educators to be consciously aware of potential talent. They must encourage the talent of children and help to strengthen their talent. Those whose talents become dormant and shrink to the point of no return have little chance of being revived. It is also of utmost importance for every family, educator, and society to recognize and to understand that every child is their responsibility and that everyone talent lost will be their unforgivable doing. Teamwork and diversity of different talents are so important for the development and progress of every working society. Working together as a team, as one functioning body where there is complete complementarily between different parts, is the key to a successful society. We must work together in concert, the same way many systems of our body work in concert to function as one healthy and productive body or system.

"Employers have recognized for some time that it's smart business to have a diverse workforce-one in which views are represented and everyone's talent are valued." - Thomas Perez

We must also understand the subject that we are talking about and its responsibility because every talent is given as a free gift that comes with great responsibility. For all those that are on the receiving side of talent, you must acknowledge that without the effort and help of family and education, society will not make any difference.

"As simple as it sounds, we all must try to be the best person we can: by making the most of the talents we have been given." Mary Lou Retton

Those that are masters of their talent need to help in a way that demonstrates right and accurate instructions about the importance of every given talent. They must teach others to know who they are and what Talent means for their life.

They must be prepared for the power they possess through their given Talent and their position and their function in this world as a responsible member of human society. They must always remember that this Talent is a free gift that comes with great responsibilities in order to do right. The purpose of talent is not to do good for ourselves but to do good for others via living in consortium, in close relation with other different incomparable talents. We may come to one common conclusion, that everyone born has the right to have the opportunity to discover and evolve their given Talent as the solid foundation for the future life of humanity.

"We must not lose faith in our Humanity."-Gandhi

We are Humanity and Humanity is our lives. To conclude, I leave you with wise insights from a few talented individuals in hopes of building a common understanding about our life and the life of humanity.

"We believe in some basic human principles-everyone should have the opportunities not just to survive, but to excel with their God given talents and

abilities. Those are the values that should be reflected in our budgets."- Patrick Kennedy.

We all have a talent and through our talent or talents we are all ONE.

"We are all connected to everyone and everything in the universe. Therefore, everything one does as an individual affects the whole. All thoughts, words, images, prayers, blessings, and deeds(by given Talents) are listened to by that is."- Serge Kahili King.

One thing is true, that America remains the one country that promotes and encourages humans Talent. This is what makes our country the lighthouse of the world. America, the land of opportunity, has a magnetic power that draws in people from around the world, giving them the opportunity to find their talents. America will continue to be a promising country for every talent not only for American's but for the entire world and for the future of all humanity.

"For generations, America has served as a beacon of hope and freedom for those outside her borders, and as a land of limitless opportunity for those risking everything to seek a better life. Their talents and contribution have continued to enrich our country"- Spencer Bachus

Nikola Tesla is a man that used his talent to its fullest potential. Born in the small village of Smiljan in former Yugoslavia, Tesla is known as one of the most talented beings, bringing light (literally and figuratively) that we have now in our country for civilian and industrial life. His talent was electricity and electromagnetism which created so many new things and opportunities, impacting the lives of those living in Europe and in America. These life altering inventions came about through the work of one talented man. His talent had the opportunity to develop and grow through the love and support of his family and education. His work allowed many to live a productive life. That is what family does. That is what proper education does. That is what a prosperous society does and that is what properly nurtured talent does-Genius.

It's all about your talent, your free gift, and how you use it throughout your life as well as what you have accomplished with your talent. This is what counts. Talent is born in families, dressed in education, indoctrinated in society and rewarded throughout the universe. We must create productive members of our national family where every member will take its given position for the benefit of all.

"What lies behind us and what lies before us are tiny matters compared to what lies within us.

Ralph Waldo Emerson.

To conclude we must say that every talented one has its own life purpose to be fulfilled to the last bit before come time for natural departure. *"I do not want to die... until I have faithfully made the most of my talent and cultivate the seed(talent is the seed) that was place in me until the last small twig has grown."- Kathe Kollwitz.*

Kollwitz knew that from good seeds come good trees and from good trees come good fruits. That is a law of nature that also rules our human life. Everything in that seed is a blue print where our entire life has been written. Our life, our life purpose, our life goal, and our life's reward. Well done and well said Kathe Kollwitz.

Every society needs members with visions to see things that other cannot in order to create a new world, for the benefit of our entire humanity. And on end for myself who arrived, to this country, as already established physician and surgeon, with my mother, with my wife and my two sons and with only 250 dollars in my pocket in the greatest country that provided opportunity for me and only opportunity for my one small talent to be and to become physician I MADE IT what was only possible in this greatest and exceptional country

It is society that must provide opportunity for every talent to advance from active talent through life experiences to the level of genius to come from the power o nature to the master of nature and move this world forward for the better life for all.

"We comprehend the Earth only when we have known heaven. Without the Spiritual world the material world is a disheartening enigma." Joseph Joubert

In order for our world to move forward we must combine material world with spiritual world in order to bring progress and better life for entire humanity. Talent is only solution to our material world to do it.

HAPPINESS IS JOY #5

Everybody is born with certain purpose what we call talent to do the best, to love what they do the best, what brings real happiness in order to become partaker in life with their given talent.

A real great talent finds its happiness in executions." Johan Wolfgang Goethe

Happiness is following your given talent as a power of love to echo toward entire humanity as we are all born to live in the circle of our life. Everyone is born with talent which has been given to us according to our personal abilities, allowing us to succeed. Skill and direction in life, along with abilities, all give us the energy needed in order to proceed and to follow our leader, our talent, which is not beneficial without ability. Similarly, one without the other is not worthy of the success needed to provide happiness. Talent is our skill, and direction with power and energy needed to proceed.

"Talent without abilities is lame and abilities without talent is blind" Dragan P. Bogunovic, MD

Working together in concert, talent and personal abilities are a powerful team. Enduring hard work is the essence of real and true happiness. Only through accomplishing our goals can we reach real genuine happiness.

"True happiness involves the full use of one's power (abilities) and talent." John W. Gardner.

The meaning behind Gardner's quote is that talent is given to every living soul, to work hard according to its abilities in order to succeed and to be happy.

"The person born with a talent they are meant to use, will find their greatest happiness in using." Johann Wolfgang von Goethe

Happiness always comes with team work with talent as its leader where your abilities playing a supportive role. Nothing good can ever be done without team work between humans talent and personal abilities.

"Your talent determines what you can do- talent is your skill- Your motivation determines how much you are willing to do. Your attitude determines how well you do it." Lou Holtz.

Talent is your love and your skill. Motivation, simply said, is your readiness and willingness to carry out your talent. Determination is equivalent to the motivation and readiness you posses which allows you to confront the many difficulties and obstacles that occur along the way. Again, determination means never giving up. Both motivation and attitude are part of your inborn ability to do work and to finish whatever you do. Your motivation and positive attitude may allow you to do well however, you will never be able to do your best without your talent, motivation and good attitude all working together. Your talent not only gives you the opportunity to fly to heavenly heights but also brings true and real happiness, a feeling that those who do not use their talent will never feel.

"You can do something extraordinary, and something that lot of people can't do. And if you have the opportunity to work on your gift-talent it seems like a crime not to do. I mean, it's just weakness to quit because something becomes too hard." - Morgan M

Without talent and the hard work involved, real lasting happiness is not possible. Talent is life's direction and a skill that requires extra power in order to endure the hard work involved. This power has been graciously instilled in each and every one of us and comes in the form of: courage, perseverance, motivation, attitude, strength and more importantly will power that never gives up which eventually leads to lasting happiness. Our talent gives us a purpose in life; this purpose is to be happy while living in the frame of the power of our given talents. Talent means nothing more or less than living your life according to your ability.

Talent is an extraordinary power that allows us to live our lives to their fullest potential as way to undivided happiness. Without our talents we cannot obtain real happiness. Which is nothing but eternal happiness.

"Happiness... consists in giving and in serving others." Henry Drumm

Serving others is the purpose of talent. Every talented being must see his talent as a gift that can be utilized to benefit for all. Talent is power of love and our connection with other talent creating unity with mutual benefits.

There is truth in Gyatso's statement. Happiness resides in each and every one of us and is dependent on our actions. If we do look for happiness, we will never find happiness. Happiness lives in our hearts and only through hard work can it yield to true happiness. Talent takes work, hard work, work whose sole purpose is to master our skill in order to do good for others. Mastering your skill means getting better and better, by growing in the power of your talent what means to never stop progressing.

Talent is all three that includes: work, loving what you do, and the desire to do good. Talent is an activity. Mastering any talent takes practice and patience. It is the power within your talent that will lead you to eternal happiness.

Talent is your love and gives you the power to practice compassion. Doing good to others as the main purpose of our talent is real way to open our heart and to let happy feeling comes out.

Our happiness dwells in our gift, our given talent. With talent comes the love of doing things in accordance to this precious gift. Talent is our love. Love and embrace who and what we are. And know that this love comes from our hearts, where happiness is born. Yes, in our heart where our talent abides and where our happiness gives birth to opportunities.

"You cannot find happiness by chasing after it. Happiness comes from doing what you love to do, and from being who you truly are." - Jonathan Lockwood Huie.

The happiness in our heart and in our mind opens upon execution, what releasing small amount of hormones from the brain as Serotonin, Endorphin producing good feelings, satisfaction, and happiness.

"Joy, satisfaction and happiness blooms where minds and hearts are open." - *Jonathan Lockwood Huie*

Our talent is part of who we truly are-our identity. Only by loving what we do can we release our inner satisfaction called happiness. Talents are actions that bring true happiness by opening our hearts as areal and true sources of our happiness.

"The joy is in the journey"- Anonymous

Discovering and mastering our given talent is our one true journey in the life. Every journey taken in right direction lead us to discover purpose of our life which is nothing but joy and happiness. Every journey is unique, bringing ups and downs which have been intentionally given to us. These is are trials and tribulations to teach us to work hard, endure challenges, to persevere, and to never give up.

"There are only two ways to live your life. One is as though nothing is miracle. The others is as though everything is a miracle." - Albert Einst

Only one will generate happiness and that way is living life as though everything is a miracle. We have our talents to guide us to miracles that are alive and all around us, to be seen and to be taken. We go our given way, facing good and bad, and conquer all those obstacles. Never give up achieving your given goal and what will deliver satisfaction and happiness.

Our talent is our most important tool-supporting and protecting us from whatever life challenges are. In every case, in every time, in every situation, we will keep dancing, happily accepting all the good and bad time that may come upon us while natural process will activate all those happy hormones coming from our brain's

Our Talent is the greatest power of love allowing us to face all possible difficulties on our path towards accomplishing of our goals.

We must take from this book the idea that what we are and what we do love comes to us through our talent. What we are doing is our talent. What we are and our love for our talents is what creates happiness. Each one of us has talent and are predestined to live a happy life. All those that are keep a close relationship with this free given gift, holding it as a personal possession in their hearts, will live every moment of their life in happiness. What we are is our talent and this makes us worthy of every good thing that brings happiness.

"Happiness is when what you think, what you say, and what you do are in harmony." Gand

Happiness is the real power that is guiding you. Directing you is the power of love from your heart. Our talent is known as the cohesive power which keeps all things together in unity. Yes, talent has the power of unity to bring all things, all talents, together in one united and healthy body; acting for the benefit ofothers to bring personal satisfaction and happiness. Talent is love and love is a miracle which every talented soul experiences day by day.

"We are all given that power of love, our talent and earned happiness, to be able to share with others the fruits of our work." Dragan P. Bogunovic, MD

"A Real great talent finds its happiness in executions." - Johann Wolfgang Goethe

We all belongs to each other and no one is ever alone as long as we have each other because, we all belong to this world as a part of a universe. We are all connected through the power of love, our talents. Talent is the power of love and serves as a connection to each other and the entire universe.

"We are all connected to everyone and everything in the universe. Therefore, everything one does as an individual affects the whole. All thoughts, words, images, prayers, blessing, and deeds are listened by all that is." Serge Kahili King.

This connection, the power of love, is our way to happiness. Our talent is love and our purpose in life where our purpose is to be happy.

We are all given a talent and must live according to our gift. We must also live and work in unity with other talents, sharing our lives and happiness together as one entity. We are created to live in unity together as brothers and sisters. We must be kind to each other and share our happiness.

"The more we care for happiness of others, the greater is our own sense of well being." Tenzin Gyatso

To conclude, we must state that: talent is love and talent is life purpose, for there is no real happiness without love and a purpose.

RELIGION#6

Everyone born upon this planet is born with a given gift called talent, and no one is excused. This is a fact. This brings us to the natural conclusion that talent is a free gift to everyone regardless of religion, race, gender, or ideology. It is a spiritual gift to everyone and speaks universal language that every living soul can hear. Its voice is recognizable and understood by all. Talent is given to and belongs to everyone. It provides a purpose in life that all can benefit from. Talent, in the beginning, is like a secular religion. It provides a good and happy life for others in society. As every talent means enduring difficulties, it becomes stronger and stronger with experience. It is through experience that our talents mature, expanding its effects by opening its horizon thus benefiting society and humanity. It can now transform from being a secular religion to a humanistic religion. Eventually, via maturation, by mastering its power it develops wings in order to rise above humanity to becoming a universal religion with new eyes. This talent evolves from pure talent to genius.

"Nature is the master of talents; genius is the master of nature." Josiah Gilbert Holland

When you master your talent and become *its* master, your talent becomes a form of genius. Now, this genius is the master of nature making your talent both earthly and Universal in the sense that it is far beyond the ground on which you stand.

"All our talents increase in the using, and every faculty, both good and bad, strengthens by exercise..." Anne Bronte

Under humanistic talent you are under the law of nature, walking according to that law.. But when you become winged, you fly high becoming a light of this world... a light of "the world"- becoming muster of the nature. The purpose of life is to recognize your talent and its power. Your personal talent possesses a certain power which can take you to the level that has been predestined for you. This level differs from person to person and is reached only through hard work.

"God gives talent. Works transforms talent into genius." - Anna Pavlova

Talent is gift that is often accompanied by challenge. If it were not challenging and void of responsibility, it won't be worth doing. Our talents are simply useless without hard work.

"Hard works pays off-hard work beats talent any day, but if you are talented and work hard, it's hard to beat." Robert Griffin III

We all must accept the truth that talent is a gift from above, a gift which was known and accepted a long time ago which presently has been forgotten. The philosophy and beliefs of talent need again to be recognized and repeated in order to better the lives of our children as well as the lives of entire humanity.

It is the known name of Bez'al-el, with the Spirit in his heart, a well known craftsman able to do art *work,* creative work, according to his given gift, *his* given talent.

"And I have filed him with the Spirit of God, with ability and intelligence, with knowledge and all craftsmanship, to devise artistic design, to work in gold, silver, and bronze, cutting stones for setting, and in carving wood, to work in every craft." Exod. 31:3-5

From the beginning of time, up to the present, many gifted people were able to shift our world, our humanity towards a better life. Mainly from those talents that reached level of universality to be call genius. We must work hard because hard work has the power to evolve our talents and abilities into higher level according to the power of given talent This all involves hard work which evolves in stages. In order to make it through the difficulties of life, you must rely on your talent and have faith in its ability to guide you through what may seem impossible. We grow and learn from previous experiences, both good and bad. Again, there is a natural power that accompanies your talent. With the help and guidance of this power, you can overcome every life's obstacles.

In the same way that muscles grow and mature with exercise, our talent matures and grows with experience.

Never ever face the world alone. Do not be afraid or ashamed to ask for help when you need it.

I always thank God for giving me this opportunity and for blessing me with this talent."- Justin Bieber.

Justin is good example how powerful talent may make your life glorious. It is god but it is not going to be easy to keep that level untouched.

"With your talent, you constantly move forward through unknown places, places of darkness that brings light and develop new eyes." Dragan P. Bogunovic- MD

For those with advanced power of given talent in a path of discover able to see thing that is not visible to others and bringing light to our dark world.

By traveling, you continue to observe all things and to acquire wisdom which is for you to develop new eyes to see things that are not visible for your fleshly eyes. Look for the light in darkness.

Those that utilize their gift and talent have the ability to see things that others may not. It is amazing how landscapes are made clear when looking through new eyes.

"Nature is the master of talents; genius is the master of nature," Josiah Gilbert Holland

Every genius belongs to a universal religion. These new eyes allow us to see and experience miracles in the same way Michelangelo was able to see an Angel in a large piece of marble.

In regards to talent, there is a long road between secular religion and universal religion.

The lives of those who support universal religion can see the miracles and good in any situation. Their eyes allow them to see the good in situations that many deem lost. Consider the case of Alexander Fleming. Alexander Fleming is responsible for 'accidentally' discovering penicillin. The power of his *eyes* continues to save the lives of many. Hungarian doctor and physiologist, Albert Szent- Gyorgyi is credited with discovering vitamin C and components/reactions of the citric acid-ascorbic acid, which saved the lives of many suffering from scurvy, which is Vitamin "C" deficiency

"Talent hits a target no one else can hit; Genius hits a target no one else can see." Arthur Schopenhauer.

Fleming and Gyorgyi are visionaries able to see things with new eyes. Both were immensely talented, beginning their careers with a focus on secular religion. Both eventually went on to support humanistic religion but shortly after became members of Universal religion, what many call genius.

I conclude encouraging all talented people to take wise directions in life.

Talent is our personal religion that reflects our performances. It is all about work and about personal responsibility to work hard to endure and to never work alone without the support of your talent. I conclude this chapter with an inspirational statement from President Abraham Lincoln:

"Whenever I do good I feel good. Whenever I do bad I feel bad. That is my religion."- President Abraham Lincoln.

Fun. #7

Life is fun for all those that are guided and directed by the power of love, their free gift called talent. After all, the synonym for talent is fun. Living and working with your talent allows you to enjoy and have fun in life which will bring you good feelings and happiness. Talent is life's direction towards a successful life and great satisfaction that brings happiness. Everything you do in accordance with your given talent is fun. There is joy in doing what you love. and what you do the best. Doing what you love brings happiness, which is the purpose of living.

"People rarely succeed unless they have fun in what they are doing." Dale Carnegie

Anything we do in life we do under the guidance of our talent. We do our best in everything, we do because we love what we do. At the same time, we experience a great deal of satisfaction or fun. Talent is fun.

"To love what you do and feel that is matters, how on earth could anything be more fun." Katherine Graham

Our talent allows us to be the best in everything we do in life, because our talent is a skill that makes whole life a much easier. Our talent is with us in everything we do making life fun. It is our talent and abilities that allow us to endure hard work. Our Talent is love and whatever we do is accomplished through love, which is fun. Only talent can provide fun for every hard working talented soul. For every talent you must work hard, be courageous, and have a fun. Everything is up to you and your attitude. A good attitude allows you to see things with optimistic eyes, all in light and bright color. You will increase your blood pressure, heart rate and adrenalin. Optimism will take away all burdens and give you the power to see your life direction and your life goal, to face it and to take it using all of the strength of your body and soul. This is all the doing of power, of your talent, which delivers good feeling we may and we will call fun.

Fun is not only a synonym of human talent but is also the consequence of every talent which endures hard work. Yes, we may call it fun but fun is a process of growing higher and higher to develop the powerful feeling of satisfaction and happiness. Talent is fun but it is also a close relative to human happiness. Consider fun as a result of accomplishing things that are in reference to your life purpose, your talent.

While watching her child, a mother beholds a happy child doing thing that that child loves (Talent). She observes her child actively playing which, to this child, is nothing more than having a good time and having fun as a projection of maturing it's given talent. She cannot see talent nor can anyone else however, she is able to see fruits of that talent which are presented in the form of a happy child, doing and playing with their entire body and soul i.e. having fun. Happiness, devotion, attitude, motivation, persistence, and perseverance are evident in every child's acting talent what will all noticeably improve with age. Many of these humans' attributes which originate in human abilities are observable as result of human born talent and activities. It is incredibly important for every mother not only to observe, but also to register every important act in accordance to their talent and ability. This will create a prosperous life for their child. Every child is brought into this world with a dream and a purpose in life. These dreams can be achieved only when we find and use our talent, our purpose.

It would be beneficial to all children, to have a list or poster in their home containing basic instructions about talent, fun, love and happiness which are all a direct result of active talent. These words of wisdom need to be spoken at home at an early age opposed to later in life when later in life when more advanced practicum will be introduced for further development of talent. These words will serve as a constant reminder that is necessary for proper advancement. Observe your children and what they are doing for fun. Always encourage them and provide all the necessary elements that will continue their appropriate advancement.

Always keep in mind that every talent is only a seed that must be placed in appropriate ground to grow. Our children need attention and support just as a seed needs care and nourishment to grow into a grand tree bearing fruit, which we will all one day be able to consume. That which is fun is fun because of the hard work we endure through our talent.

"When you have confidence you can have a lot of fun. And when you have fun, you can do amazing thing." Joe Namath

Trusting your talent and following its lead is a sign of complete confidence which will lead to success and happiness. One of most important things to remember is that you need to constantly remind your children to practice their talent as they grow and mature. Remind them that joy and fun should never be ceased as long as they live and practice their talent for the entirety of their lives.

"Even though you are growing up, you should never stop having fun." Nina Dobrev

Secondly, we must note that whatever you do must be done out of love while having fun otherwise, you are not working in accordance of your talent. Remember that the work of talent is always love and always provides fun. No love means no fun and no fun is not the work of your given talent. There is potential in children who know how to play with their gift, love it, and have fun playing. Through play and fun, their love and talent will never stop growing. That is a process that all children experience. They act spontaneously from their heart, where love is and where their given gift, their talent abides. Every parent should observe their child's activities and understand what is going on in order to be able to support and to encourage their child. It is necessary to relay this information to their teachers who will then provide the child with the proper care and education needed. This care should be individualized according to every child's unique and specific needs but also needs to embrace that child's talent and ability. Only then will our children's talent develop and mature.

Not every talent is the same nor does every child possess only one talent. Every child is granted at least one talent which will give them the opportunity to become active and productive members of society. Their participation is critical for the development of society. I am certain that every parent, teacher, and every member of our society will have the greatest pleasure observing and following the progress of every born talented human soul. We must also say that the continuing progress of one talented soul will provide much eternal fun. The effects of their talent are evident from day one and continue throughout their education. The fruits of their talent are both rich and inexhaustible and when combined with other talents, has the ability to eliminate hunger throughout society. This is the purpose of talent. We have all been blessed with unparalleled talents for one purpose: to unite our talents for the benefit of society. I am particularly fond of Ms. Nina Dobrev her thoughts on life so, I leave you, once again, with her wise words:

"Even though you are growing up, you should never stop having fun." - Nina Dobrev

Having fun and enjoying life are all a part of living however, we must ask why is life fun and what does our gift have to do with life and the fun we experience? I have meditated and thought about the answer to that question and have come to follow conclusions:

1) Life is fun for all those that are guided and directed by the power of love, their given free gift called talent because we can all agree that the synonym for talent is fun.

2) Living, working, and having fun through and with your talent is what brings us good feelings and happiness. Talent is life's direction towards a successful and satisfying life filled with happiness.

3) Everything you do in accordance to your given talent is fun because talent is equivalent to fun.

There is joy in doing what you love and POWER in your personal abilities to do the best which will undoubtedly lead you to everlasting happiness, which is our purpose of our life.

When we do right and love what we do, it is fun that brings us happiness. Fun is the reward of our talent. Our love of our talent is a power that allows us to find happiness in everything we do.

Many of us dream about talent and often wonder about its role. In order to explain this, I will use the analogy of driving a car. Talent is a given skill such as the skill needed to drive and operate a car in a safe way. However, in order to drive car we must have skill but also need to have a car to drive. In other words, we may have talent but our talent is useless unless we use it.

We cannot do anything with our talent without support from our personal abilities which differ from person to person. Talent is our skill and our car is our personal abilities what we have in order to drive a car.

We cannot use our talent without support from our personal abilities just as we cannot drive if there is no car to drive.

Talent is our skill while our abilities (courage, perseverance, endurance, and motivation)are all attributes used to support and build our skill. Just as a car does not move without a skilled driver, our talent does not move without ability. Now, certain abilities may allow us to perform random tasks but keep in mind, these tasks are nominal when compared to what we can do with our talent and ability to carry out that talent. In other words, it is possible to drive a car without the necessary skills however, you are jeopardizing your life and the lives of other drivers.

"It is good to have an end to journey, but it is the journey that matters in the end." Ursula. Le Guin

It is talent and personal ability that matters through our journey; talent is nothing without ability and our ability reflects upon our talent.

"Hard works pays off-hard work beats talent any day, but if you are talented and work hard it is hard to beat."

R. Griffin

Life is fun because of the journey.

Using car for driving as a modus operandi with picturesque presentation to depict importance of human's talent and it's so close relation with human's abilities and dependence for the real human life, life of happiness and fun in same way as you drive a car over the beautiful land scenery what really makes you happy to have a great deal of fun. Driving car through beautiful countryside or going through life guided and directed by your given power, your talent is joy, satisfaction and fun what causes true happiness. Or we may use our river of life as one of the best ways to presents importance of our talents and our personal abilities.

River of life as one best way to presents importance of our talent and our personal abilities.

"River of life moves without apparent purpose. It moves slowly without any resistance what every human souls would enjoy moving forward slowly without any resistance. Go slowly down with river, surrender to the flow of the river of life but do not flow down like a log, but float down with the time without resisting nor to hurry becoming your rudder your talent with together of your energy your power your personal abilities to direct and correct your course and avoid all possible obstacles on a way to the end of your path." That must be great experience great satisfaction and on first place fun flowing down with the power of your river of life.

Talent is given as our life purpose to float down the river of our life slowly and directed by our talent and supported by our inborn abilities with satisfaction and fun to the very end of our life path. Use it because it is all yours and for your life to have a fun and to find in it your happiness which is all in you and in your way to float slowly through life like river does.

Team work "8

My Inspiration for this chapter comes from individuals whose thoughts and theories continue to impact this world, our world, your world. Their combined wisdom encourages us to create and support a form unity where every human member of society can come together to better our society and world.

"Never doubt that a small group of thoughtful committed people can change the world. Indeed, it is the only thing that ever has." Margaret Mead.

It is critical for us all to come together and utilize our individual talents; as a whole, our talents are complimentary making one talent as essential as the next one. There is power in numbers, and together our talents have the power to change the world by creating a better society, a society that has a place for everyone.

"Individual commitment to a group effort-that is what makes team work, a company work, a society work, a civilization work." Vince Lombardi

Each member of every team has a specific role that is needed in order to make the team successful. Discover your talent and let that serve as your motivator. This motivation will guide you, void of procrastination and weaving, to the end of its predetermined path.

Unity, complementarities, and common goals are all conceived from common people. They make up one powerful body which is able to realize 'uncommon commitments' known to some as a miracle. This is done through the power of natural or even supernatural law where two together may lift more than two separated. Consider the philosophy that one and one is not two but three. This is a law of nature that serves as the source of power that every team can generate. Again, there is strength and power in numbers demonstrating that we are stronger as a team opposed to be separated.

Walter Disney's creation of Disneyland serves as an exceptional example of the power and effectiveness of teamwork. Disney gathered together many different talents, but complimentary to each others', and was able to build an empire which was coordinated by the vision of their leader, Mr. Walter Disney.

Living, working, and creating together is the essence of human life. When we collaborate together, we are stronger as well as more likely to find our purpose in life. Unity guarantees peace and prosperity.

"Individually, we are one drop. Together, we are ocean. Ryunosuke Satoro

Team work is founded upon human talent, where different people with different talents become one solid body. Everyone has his own talent which functions to create one solid and healthy body. Consider the human body; there are so many different parts with different functions being united and complimentary to create one strong and healthy body. That is the way of nature and a law of our humans existence.

"A dream you dream alone is only a dream. A dream you dream together becomes reality." John Lennon

It is true that all those members of every team become one body one soul and one spirit living, thinking, dreaming, and making dreams come true together. Talent is a free gift that when combined with other talents, allows us to fulfill our every dream. Uniting our talent with others' creates a powerful productive machine where every gear turns on its own but is dependent on every other gear in order to fulfill its purpose.

"Teamwork is so important that it is virtually impossible for you to reach the heights of your capabilities or make any profit that you want without becoming very good at it". Brian Tracy

Team work presents a future for every society that works hard to invent and to prosper for the entire society. Teamwork is the power of creating new things for a new life that brings prosperity for many to rejoice in. There is no success without team work.

"Coming together is a beginning; keeping together is progress; working together is success." Henry For

Henry Ford also believe as Walter Disney did, in human talent and even more in those talents working together as a team, creating a powerful body realize his dream that his talent dreams.

Both Walter Disney and Henry Ford as well as many others lived their dreams through their many different talents acting as one body, as one productive team. Their talents and dreams served the world and were a benefit for entire humanity. No one soul has been denied on a basis of skin color nationality, language, religion, and many others humans differences.

That is the work of every talent that is nothing but the love for all and for the goodness for entire world.

Teamwork performs in same way as an orchestra where many different instrument play different music to create beautiful sounds and harmony, pleasing for many. They all play together but are directed by one person, the conductor, to bring them all in one sound, in one glorious harmony.

That beautiful harmony is the result of team work where, every action is blessed to succeed that please many listeners.

"You don't get harmony when everybody sings the same song." Doug Floyd

Different people and different talents sing together, creating one beautiful sound. Teamwork is a creation that starts from one talented leader who gathers many different talents, for many different positions to build a body that will guarantee to work as one perfectly designed machine where every gear moves alone and in same time together in concert with others.

Everything is created according to the vision of leaders and his/her dream. A dream or vision is the beginning but is dependent on two more important parts. Hard work is necessary in order to gain experience and improve that talent.

The second piece involves the ability to work and collaborate with others in order to use your talent to its fullest ability. Team progress moves forward and only works when its members treat one another as a family.

Teamwork is nothing new, it is a well known entity that is so complicated and so difficult to start, organize and to lead.

First, every team needs a talented leader that is a dreamer with a vision to gather together different talents for different positions where all are able to do their work and at the same time to work close in consortium with others. That unity must be lived, ensuring that everybody comprehends the importance and seriousness of hard work.

Improving your talent is just as important as working hard. Improving means constantly growing and maturing constantly offering a better and better performance all together.

Using the example of a soccer team, the team manager is responsible for every action and every difficult decision needed to be made. His actions are needed in order for that unity to move forward every day and acts to benefit the entire program purpose. It is one powerful, living entity that needs constant care in every second of their action in order to succeed.

There is no real team without a talented leader and talented members to act daily to be responsible to governing the body who is in charge for that teamwork.

"Leadership is based on inspiration, not domination; on cooperation, not intimidation."

William Arthur Ward.

Here, William Arthur Ward is speaking about everything involved in leadership and management of a team. Every good organized team has the potential for proper development and success because all those talents are granted the ability to work All in All.

We must all be thankful to all those talented people for the things that we all have in common, that bring us all together because, all those good and common things far outnumber and out weight those that divide us.

It is the power of our unique individual human talents that has that cohesive power to bring unity and peace to our humanity.

We must always remember that power of our love our given talent is peace and unity.

END

Conclusion. #9

Talent is given to every living person with the purpose of achieving happiness and doing good.

Talent is our life, our life direction and our life purpose, which is to be happy.

Every talent should be discovered and is born out of a loving family. It is nurtured by the unconditional love of mothers.

Every mother should or rather, must be informed prior to motherhood about the importance of their roles and responsibilities in regards to the future of their children.

Yes, there are many mothers responsibilities but one that is most important for the future of their children is their future life, their destiny, that will continue even after mother is not any more around to help.

It is the responsibility of our medical society to inform every pregnant women about the responsibilities of motherhood awaiting her.

Similar to this book, we must create a book of short instructions and insight for all mothers to reference because the future of that newborn child is the future of our society.

This book entails important information however, I am conscious that this is not going to be enough. The intention of this book is not to teach but rather, to give incite to every mother, every educator, and every responsible part of our society; to add on and to develop complete programs which will guaranty full development of our future members of society.

A child exhibiting a lack of interest and desire in education is a sign that they are neglecting their talent. This child is certainly not without talent but lacks guidance and the knowledge of the importance of finding God's given talent. In such cases, we must act promptly to correct this lack of guidance and motivation.

This book was written with good intentions for every newborn child. I firmly believe that is true that every talent is truly a free gift that must be developed for each child to become powerful leader of their future. Today, December 11, 2014 is the day I officially completed this book with the intention to do good and benefiting every newborn living soul. I also believe, as a former medical officer, that this is my ethical duty. I have, in my 50 years of medical practice, saved many human lives and know in my heart that every human soul can be saved by properly acting on its talent. It is through our talent that we can live a life of true happiness. - z

"I do not want to die... until I have faithfully made the most of my talent and cultivated the seed that was place in me until the last twig has grown." Kathe Kollwitz

I must admit that I love talent because talent belongs to every soul and does not discriminate based on skin color, language, religion, birth place, sexuality or political orientation.

We must find our talent and do what we love or we run the risk of doing nothing at all.

Talent belongs to everyone and loves everyone which is why I love TALENT.

"Refuse to be average. Let your heart soar as high as it will." Alden Wilson Tozer.

"Open your heart and let your talent free to soar as high as its given power." - Dragan P. Bogunovic

In order to succeed, you must trust your given gift, your talent, believing in its power, without any doubt, to take you in the right life direction meant for you.

We must all recognize and take this from this small book, the idea that your life, your destiny, is in your hands and heart. Belief is your main source of power which allows you to act, without any doubt.

"Believe in yourself, in your vision for your future and in your ability to take a small step each day forward achieving your vision." Jonathan Lockwood Huie

It is your life and your destiny to take it and live happy life.

This book is created off the visions of all those famous and successful people whose names still live in our memories. Their visions are to be trusted and to be followed, because talent and hard work gives meaning to our lives but also allows us to live in peace with ourselves and with others.

Practice #1

Every man grows during difficult time by enduring as a main stimulating factor for humans development in endurance.

1. *"Nothing splendid has ever been achieved except by those who dared believe that something inside of them was superior to circumstances."* Bruce Barton

They achieved because they endured which is growing through life to be able to endure as superior toward life circumstances

2. *"What lies behind us and what lies before us are tiny matters compared to what lies within us." Ralph Waldo Emerson.*

Main part of our abilities that we are born with and what needs to be aggrandize is our endurance. Agree?

3. *"The boldness of endurance is the underline to almost every success."*

Mary Anne Radmacher

Talent is skill and cannot produce without power of endurance to sustain all difficulties on a way. You may be very skill in playing tennis but you must endure entire time before success. Agree?

4. *"Nothing great was ever done without much enduring."* Catherine of Siena

Way to success is through much enduring.

And there is no way to learn endurance other than simple to endure. Agree?

5. *"Not in achievement but in endurance of the human soul, does it show its divine grander and its alliances with the infinitive."* Edwin Hubbel Chapin

Endurance is testing for every human soul to resist and never give up because you are never alone in this world. Agree?

6. *"The firs virtue in a solder is endurance of fatigue, courage is only the second virtue."* Napoleon Bonaparte.

Endurance is part of humans abilities but also is the great virtue for life of many humans soul develop in time of national crisis. Agree?

7. *"Endurance is not just the ability to bear a hard thing, but to turn it into glory."*

William Barclay.

When one endure to never give up but endure to the end for the glory. Because endurance is divine grandeur connected with infinitive. Agree?

8. *"What is to give light must endure burning."* Eleanor Roosevelt/

There is no victory-light without burning-darkness. Darkness is only absence of light and as soon light comes there is no darkness, because light is stronger than darkness

When you bring light to darkness then there is no more darkness and not otherwise

Agree?

Next 10 are all about COURAGE that is what carry every Talents action from beginning up to the very end. Without courage there is no beginning nor Talent act.

1. *"There are risk and cost to action. But they are far less than the long range risk of comfortable inaction."* John F. Kennedy

Talent is action and courage heart is decision to act. Agree?

2. *"Corage and perseverance have a magic talisman, before which difficulties disappears and obstacles vanish into air."* John Quincy Adams.

Those two most important parts of human abilities are greatest power to carry every talents action toward success. Agree?

3. *"The cave you fear to enter holds the treasure you seek." Joseph Campbell*

Talent is your power for discovery things that are hidden in dark and unknown places and only with courageous heart you will be able to succeed. Agree?

4. *"Nothing in life is to be feared, it is only to be understood. Now is the time to understand more, so that we may fear less. Marie Curie*

When you gain in knowledge you in same time lose fear of something that is unknown. Many great people succeed in life by gaining knowledge and losing fear. Agree?

5. *"Life shrinks or expands in proportion to one's courage." Anais Nin*

In life it is better to be lion for one day then a sheep all your life.

Be prudent. Be right which is neither being bravado nor cowardly. Agree?

6. *"Have the courage to follow your heart and intuition. They somehow already know what you truly want to become." Steve Jobs*

You have your talent to follow in action that needs courageous heart. Without courageous heart your talent is worthless. Agree?

10. *"I learned that courage was not the absence of fear, but the triumph over it. The brave man is not he who does not feel afraid, but he who conquers that fear."*

Nelson Mandela.

We all have a fear but we must also be able to gather courage to conquer that fear.

Agree?

7. *"Courage doesn't always roar. Sometimes courage is the quiet voice at the end of the day saying. "I will try again tomorrow." May Anne Radmacher*

Never give up Your courage is with you all the time that only need to be call. Agree?

This part is devoted to human's PERSISTENCE.

1. *"Being defeated is often a temporary condition. Giving up is what makes it permanent."* Marilyn vos Savant.

Defeat is never permanent for those that are able to persist. Agree?

2. *"Great works are performed not by strength but by perseverance."*

Samuel Johnson

Success is equal to perseverance. Agree?

3. *"Never give up, for that is just the place and time that the tide will turn."*

Harriet Beecher Stowe.

Real persistence is to endure to the very end and never before. Agree?

4. *"I do not think that there is any other quality so essential to success of any kind as the quality of perseverance. It overcome almost everything, even nature."*

John Rockefeller

It is decisive power for every talented action. Agree?

5. *"A little more persistence, a little more effort, and what seemed hopeless failure may turn to glorious success."* Elbert Hubbard

Persistence is power to work effective to the end of the path where reward is waiting for your success. That is what we call perseverance. Agree?

6. *"The habit of persistence is the habit of victory."* Herbert Kauf

That is habit that needs practice that needs to keep repeating in order to become your nature your habit. Agree?

7. *"Success is to be measured not so much by the position that one has reached in life as by the obstacles which he has overcome."* Booker T. Washington

It is not about easy life but with number and difficulties from obstacles is measure of one's power of perseverance. Agree?

8. *"A man who is a master of patience is master of everything else."* George Sav

Being patient is also being persistent. One without otter is not working. That is so natural like every natural way that says: Nature does not hurry, yet everything is accomplish. Patience and perseverance is nature. Agree?

Following about MOTIVATION.

1. *"Life must be lived and curiosity kept alive. One must never, for whatever reason, turn his back on life."* Eleanor Roosevelt

Life is continue perpetual movement that only those that are motivated well will continue without turning back on life. Agree?

2. *"A little more persistence, a little more effort, and what seemed hopeless failure may turn to glorious success."* Elbert Hubb

To never give up what means being motivate to accomplish in spite of so many impassable obstacles. All those difficult obstacles are daily phenomenon that we must overcome and only by power of being motivated to do it and to do right. Motivation always leads to persistence. Agree?

3. *"Opportunity dances with those already on the floor."* H. Jackson Brow

Like every morning bath will make you ready for dancing with every opportunity that comes on dancing floor. Dance every day as practicing motivation day by day without stopping. Agree?

ATTITUDE as a way of response that may go either way good or bad mostly base on humans abilities and experience that with time has tendency to change. Way how to act is result of humans attitude or not in every case?

1. *"Attitude is everything." Charles Swind*

There are many different components how one is going to react-respond. However for those that are guide by their talents is the stimuli how to act or react?

Agree?

2. *"The greatest discovery of any generation is that a human being can alter his life by altering his attitude." William James.*

Now we are talking of changing our attitude by developing new experience or knowledge. Again may go either way good or bad where talent is always a good way. Agree?

3. *"A happy person is not a person in a certain set of circumstances, but rather a person with a certain set of attitudes." Hugh Down*

Facing different type of circumstances your attitude may change in many different ways, being happy or not happy. Agree?

4. *"The talent for being happy is appreciating and liking what you have, instead of what you don't have." Woody Allen.*

Even that is way you do respond but also that is your talent with positive attitude that leads you in right direction. But talent is happy direction even that is also endurance and hard work that is main element of happy feeling of something positive achieving. Agree?

5. *"Nothing can stop the man with the right mental attitude from achieving his goal nothing on earth can help the man with wrong mental attitude."* Thomas Jefferson.

Way of your achievement declare your attitude. If everything goes well keep it, but if things are going bad changed. Agree?

6. *"Excellence is not a skill it is an attitude." Ralph Marston*

It is the best criteria for everyone to keep it and to follow it in any case good or not.

Agree?

7. *"Success or failure in business is caused more by the mental attitude even than mental capacity."* Walter Scott.

It is great advice for those successful to keep it and those that fail to change it.

Agree?

8. *"My attitude is never to be satisfied, never enough, never."* Duke Ellingt

No one should be because it is like everything that needs to be practice and practice until your attitude and whatever you are doing as part of your inner capacity your ability that needs to grow together with you. Never give up and treat everyone with highest respect-love. Agree?

Success belongs to those that NEVER GIVE UP

1. *"The only one who can make you give up is yourself."* Sidney Sheldon

We go back to personal attitude toward your life purpose to act with all your abilities and positive attitude to never ever give up toward your goal. Agree?

2. *"Never give up on the most important goals in your life. Never give up on your life purpose. Never give up on your core values."* Jonathan Lockwood

That all is in your heart where your love is and where your talent abides as your life goal and your life purpose as your core values is. Agree?

3. *"Circumstances do not defeat you-you defeat yourself when you give up."*

Jonathan Lockwood Huie.

When circumstances step on your way you must endure and persevere as result of positive attitude toward your life purpose. Agree?

4. *"Most people give up just when they are about to achieve success. Ross Perot*

You will never know when is right time to give up and for that simple reason you should never, never give up. Agree?

5. *"We cannot always choose our external circumstances, but we can always choose how to respond to them."* Epicritus

That is real attitude that whenever situation is in action to never give up.

When you are on a way to accomplish your given goal no external circumstance will make you to give up. Agree?

Now is the time for ENCOURAGING.

I personal believe that there is nothing in this world that can encourage man like it's given power. power of love it's given talent.

1. *"Individually, we are one drop. Together, we are an ocean."* Satoro

Unity is not only way to success but also power of encouragement.

2. *"Choose your life purpose and excel at living into purpose." Jonathan Lockwood.*

Talent is your given life purpose to live and to fulfill your given gift-gift of life. Agree?

OPPORTUNITY is our open door for our activity toward our life purpose.

1. *"Opportunity multiply as they are seized."* *Sun Tzu*

Those they are directed by their given talent are those that are intensively looking for every chance for every open door to enter for every opportunity either small or big. Agree?

2. *"Small opportunity are often the beginning of great enterprises."* *Demosthenes*

No one can tell you about small or big opportunity because every opportunity is opportunity to become big one. Everyone is our chance to do make a big. Agree?

3. *"The world is all gates, all opportunities, string of tension waiting to be struck."*

Ralph Waldo Emerson.

Where ever you look you may see something as a possible gates to be enter as a chance as a opportunity for life. Agree?

4. *"Wise men make more opportunities then they find."* Francis bacon

It is wisdom to find opportunity in places they do not appears as to be. If you do look out may be that one right one, because in this case wisdom is only being attentive. Agree?

5. *"Our opportunities to do good are our talents."* Cotton Mather

Talent is our life opportunity our life purpose for one and only one reason to do good. Agree?

6. *"A pessimist is one who makes difficulties of his opportunities and an optimist is one who makes opportunities of his difficulties."* Harry S. Truman

Everything is in beholders eyes. Or better to say about your attitude being positive or negative. Agree?

7. *"If you wait for opportunities to occur you will be one of the crowd."*

Edward

Talent never waits. Talent looks and if there is no opportunity Talent has power to create every opportunity to be taken and to be turn in success. Agree?

COMPASSION is life of every talented man because talent is power of love and compassion.

1. *"If you want other to be happy, practice compassion. If you want to be happy, practice compassion."* *Tenzin Gyatso-14th Dalai Lama*

Practicing compassion is same as sun shine upon you to both side That is expression of love and our Talents are power of love from our hearts. Agree?

2. *"The best way to cheer yourself is to try to cheer someone else."* *Mark Twai*

It is all about compassion which is expression of love and care to others. Talent loves and does every work for others goodness. Agree?

3. *"The more we care for the happiness of others, the more is our own sense of well-being."* Tenzin G

Loving attitude toward others is what makes your heart happy one. That is like sunrays reflect for one to other as a worm feeling. Agree?

4. *"No one can find inner peace except by working, not in self-centered way, but for the whole human family."* Peace

Trough giving we do receive internal peace and happiness, where giving is expression of love toward yours human family what keeps humanity together. Compassion comes from heart which is power of love. Agree?

5. *"To know even one life has breathed easier because you have lived. That is succeeded."* *Ralph Waldo Emerson.*

That is all about talent as a power of love from heart to work for the benefits of many. Talent is love and is also feeling of compassion for others. Agree?

For those that believe that TALENT IS SPIRITUAL GIFT

1. *"Every child comes with the message that God is not yet discouraged of man."*

Rabindr

Every child arrives to this land with gift in its heart free given talent as a future life given purpose, to take its place in predicted vocational places creating one organized society. Agree?

2. *"Talent is a gift which God has given us secretly, and which we reveal without perceiving."* Charles Montesquieu

Talent is the gift which is given not secretly what would be in darkness but in light because God is light and not darkness and not everybody perceive that gift, and not everybody open that gift to be able to perceive and to become part of their life. That is what we are doing now publicizing that powerful gift that everyone perceive and use it for the good for entire humanity. Agree?

3. *"Thank God for the creative ideas that enrich life by adding your own creative contribution to human progress."* Wilfred Peterson.

Everyone is given power of talent to continue creative work that has been started long time ago. For that reason we must all take that gift and work together for the farther contribution of human progress, which in any way is so slow because not so many have it to be able to contribute their given part.

4. *"I can't believe that God put us on this earth to be ordinary"* Lou Holtz

For those that discover and open their gift to do accordingly are not ordinary as those that never open their heart and become lost in their vain life. Agree?

5. *"God depends on us. It is through us that God is achieved."* Andre Gide

Through our free given gift, our talent God is continue its original creative work.

Agree?

6. *"God can only do for you what He can do through you."* Eric Butterwort

Trough you, through your given talent and through your inborn abilities, through all those that are talented He works All In All. Agree?

7. *"A winner is someone who recognize his God-given talents, works his tail off to develop them into skills, and uses these skills to accomplish his goal."* Larry

It is our humans given life opportunity to live real life. Agree?

8. *"Whatsoever we beg of God. let us also work for it."* Jerem

Talent is not only our channel for God's given purpose but also hard work to attain all given purpose. Agree?

9. *"When I stand before God at the end of my life, I would hope that I would not have a single bit of talent left, and say." I used everything you give me."*

Emma Bombeck

Talent is given to be use and to be utilized to the last bit of its power in order for promise to be realized in full without any residual in given gifts power.

Agree?

#10. *"Refuse to be average. Let your heart soar as high as it will."* Alden Wilson Tozer.

Open your heart and let your talent free to soar as high as its given power. Agree?

There are so many wise sentences directed toward God's way and our life with given gift our talent and for doing things for others what we must take in consideration and to do our the best.

Talent is love.

Practice.# 2.

101. *"There is no such things as a great talent without great will power,* "Honor de Balzac

Talent is your life direction and your will power is your engine on a way. Agree?.

102. *"I would like to be remember as someone who did the best she could with the talent she had."*

I.K. Rowing.

Every Talent has its power to be used in time as long as that powerful battery last. Agree?

103. *"Hard work pays off-hard work beats Talent any day, but if you are Talented and work hard it is hard to beat."* R. Griffin

Talent is enduring hard work where combination of human's ability and human's talent work in concert creating the best result. Agree?

104/*" Never believe that a few caring people cannot change the world. For, indeed, that is all who ever have."* Margaret Mead.

Talented people working together as a team are able to create new world. Different Talent working together in unity being complimentary to each other is guaranty for success. Agree?

105. *Individually we are one drop. Together we are ocean."* Ryunosuke Santoro

United different Talents as a working team create power called ocean.

Look at every hospital where many different talents work together being complimentary to each other for on goal. To save life. They are power they are ocean. Agree?.

Your Talent brings meaning to your entire life. Talent is your life, your life purpose and your life direction. Agree?

106. *"He who would accomplish much must sacrifice much."* James Allen.

"Nothing great was ever done without much enduring." Catherina of Siena. Agree?

107. *"Listen to the compass of your heart. All you need lies within you."* Mary Anne Radmacher

Talent is in your heart your compass your direction on a way. Listen carefully. Agree?

108. *"There are so many free occupations in our world for many different Talents to occupy."*

Each Talent has its own vocational place, predicted by the given talent, as a life occupation.

Agree?

109. *"If we wait for the moment where everything is ready, we shall never begin."* Ivan Turgenev

You Talent is always ready. Are you ready? Agree?

110. *"To go beyond is as wrong as to fall short."* Confucius

Keep your place in society according to your given Talent. Taking higher place than you deserve brings misery to the world. Agree?

111. *"Life is not about finding yourself. Life is about creating yourself."* George Bernard Shaw.

Life is about developing your Talent from being secular to being humanistic to become universal. You grow and you become old, but talent never get old but only mature. Agree?

112. *"It is only with the heart that one can see rightly; what is essential is invisible to the eyes."*

Antoine de Saint-Exupery

That must be all about spiritual eyes that are able to see what is invisible to our eyes. Agree?.

113. *"The heart is always right - if there's question of choosing between the mind and the heart-because mind is a creation of the society, not by existence. The heart is unpolluted. "*Osho

That again difference between spiritual power and human's flesh. Between mortal and immortal. Agree?

114. *"All that is real is seen with the heart."* Vivian Greene

All what is about feelings, as emotion or even to be call intuition which is outside from reason

Agree?

115. *"The way is not in the sky. The way is in the heart."* The Buddha

Always look in your heart because whatever you need is already given to you and it is in your heart. Looking toward sky will not work but your given Talent which in your heart is ready anytime. It must be true as they say; For what you pray you must go and do yourself. Agree?

116. *"Everyone should carefully observe which way his heart draws him, and then choose that way with all his strength."* Hasidic Proverb

Talent is your life direction. love it and follow it because that all is about loving what you doing

Talent is in your heart and loving what you are doing is your Talent. Love is your certainty.

Agree?

117. *Life is really simple, but we insist on making it complicated."* Confucius.

We are all born with our abilities that are already endowed and ready for action. And your given gift your Talent to cooperate together as one power for making your life simple and productive. Agree?

118. *"There's difference between knowing the path and walking the path."* Morpheus in the movie The Matrix.

Talent is your direction your love that you only need to follow. That all goes from your heart.

Agree?

119. *"As we work to create light for others we naturally light our own way."* Mary Anne Radmacher

Talent is your burning light that you need only to bring fuel regularly and to light up life for others what your talent's purpose is to fulfill your own purpose. Agree?

120. *"You can create miracles in your own life, and in the life of those around you - because you are miracle, and you are connected to the sources of all miracles."* Jonathan Lockwood Huie

That is progress of your Talent that slowly mature to become sources of all miracles. Agree?

121. *"You are what you do, not what you say you will do."* Carl Jung

You are what you talent is and what your talent does. Agree?

122. *"He who lives in harmony with himself lives in harmony with the Universe."* Marcus Aurelius

Living with yourself is living with your talent who originate from universe. That is what makes every Talent power by itself. Agree?

123. *"One must marry one's feeling to one's belief and ideas. That is only probably the only way to achieve a measure of harmony in one's life."* Napoleon Hills

It is marriage it is close relations between your abilities and your given Talent. Agree?

124. *"Spend time every day listening to what your muse is trying to tell you."* Bartholomew

If you listen carefully with open mind you may receive so many different beneficial ideas. Agree?

125.' *In this world there is always danger for those who are afraid of it."* George Bernard Shaw

Every Talent has encouraging power that leads to new discovery and to the new world. It is true because fear do not exist until is born into your life. Courage always belongs to talented one. Agree?

126. *"We have only this moment sparkling like a star in our hand - and melting like a snowflake."*

Marie B. Ray

Be aware of the moment for the opportunity that comes suddenly like lightening star and also quickly melts like snowflake. Opportunity opens the door that always close in the moment. Agree?

127. *"We believe in some basic human principles - everyone should have the opportunity not just to survive, but to excel with their God-given talents and abilities. Those are the value that should be reflected in our budgets. "*Patrick

We must trust our society to do just according to those words of social wisdom. Agree?

128. *Nature is master of talents; genius is the master of nature "*J. G. Holland

Talents are followers of natural principles from seed to the tree fruits. Genius is free to act from natural principles creating new ones.

129. *"We can't take credit for our talents. It is how we use them that counts."* Madeleine L'Engle

It is our purpose to use talent as our personal purpose in life. Talent on first place is made to be used properly in predicted time without procrastination as long as talent is in lasting power.

130. *"Unhappiness is the best defined as the difference between our talents and our expectation."?*

That must be some defect in the nature because every talent is given according to persons ability to fit like key to lock. It is like growing tree with many, many brunches but very little fruits. In that case personal desire do not fit toward their personal abilities producing some health or growing difficulties. Agree?

Most talents work as a team workers bringing great success being complementary to each other by working in unity. Agree?

131. *"Stand tall. Stand proud. Know that you are unique and magnificent. You do not need the approval; of others."* "Jonathan Lockwood Huie.

Your talent is your uniqueness. Agree?

132. *"Innovation distinguish between a leader and a follower.""* Steve Jobs.

Your talent is your leadership. Do according to your given gift. Be the leader. Agree?

133. *"Inspiration is a guest that does not willingly visit the lazy."* Pyotr Tchaikovsky

It is you talent. It is your hard work being visited by beneficial inspirations day by day. Agree?

134. *"Inspiration usually comes during work, rather than before it."* Madeleine L'Engle

Inspiration is idea that only those that work hard may make it reality. Agree?

135. *"Hard work brings prosperity, but he that follows vain person shall have poverty."* Pro

Work hard and become leader. Proverb. Agree

136. *"All children are artist. The problem is how to remain an artist once we grow up."*

Pablo Picasso

It is all in family, education and society to work together for one goal to educated Talent and to be accepted and supported in society.

Discover your Talent, work hard to become who you are, and do the work that you are, and everything will be done well and will stand solid for a long time. Agree?

137. *"The value of a man should be seen in what he gives and not in what he is able to receive."*

Albert Einstein

Talent leads in action to provide services for others. It is only one way of living, that never stops nor return back. Agree?

Living with your Talent is living rightly. You must living rightly with your Talent because your

Talent is your life. Agree?

138. *"All humans are also dream being. Dreaming ties all mankind together."* J. Kerouac

We all dream but only Talent brings us together in united work. Agree?

139. *"Powerful Dream Inspire Powerful Action."* Jonathan Lockwood Huie

Every real dream is selective dream that is dreaming according to power of available Talent.

Otherwise it is not dream but only fantasy. Agree?

140. *"No idea is so outlandish that should not be considered with a searching."* Winston Churchill

Your idea your dreams will be always considered by Talent to act or not. Every idea talent place on scale to measure reality of your dream for success. Everything is organized and work in order

Agree?

141. *"Life is not about waiting for the storm to pass. It is about learning to dance in the rain."*

Vivian

For dancing in the rain you have your dancing partner your Talent. Talent is power to dance whether in the rain or not. Agree?

142. *"Treat those that are good with goodness. Talent does. Treat those that are not good with goodness.-Talent does."* Lao Tzu.

Talent is power of love and power of goodness itself. Agree?

143. *"Follow what you are genuinely passionate about and left that guide you to your destination."*

D. Sawyer

Talent is your direction and destination. Follow it passionate. Agree?

144. *"The miracle is not that we do this work, but that we are happy to do it."* Mother Teresa

"If you love what you are doing what talent is, you will be not only successful but also happy one. Agree?

145. *"Make your work to be in keeping your purpose."* Leonardo de Vinci

Talent is your life and your life purpose. Agree?

146. *"No one save us but ourselves. No one can and no one may. We ourselves must walk the path."*

The Buddha

Talent has power to rise all our protective attributes on our way through our life path. Some are the part of our personal abilities and some we like courage develop through our life.

Because all those attributes are founded on power of love, power of love is our Talent. Agree?

147. *"Go within every day and find the inner strength so that the world will not blow your candle out."*

"K. Dunham

Talent is like burning flame that needs constant activity and regular filling with the necessary power where power is light to cover places of darkness. Do not turn of your light." Agree?

148. *"I really believe that everyone has a Talent, ability or skill that he can mine to support himself and to succeed in life."* Dean Koontz

Talent is the skill and ability is engine where both together present power for creative progressive purposes providing good not only for self but mainly for others. Agree?

149. *Do not let your fear be in the way of your dreams."* Anonymous

Keep dreaming and let your Talent do the work. Agree?

150. *"We must not lose faith in our humanity."* Gandhi

We are humanity and humanity is our lives. Agree?

151. *"I find the harder I work the more luck seems to have."* Thomas Jeffers

There is no luck but only endure hard work with your powerful talent. Agree?

152. *"The secret of our success is that we never give up."* Wilma Mankiller

It is power of our talent that persevere. AGREE?

153. *"As we let our light shine, we unconsciously give other people permission to do the same."*

Marianne Williamson

Use your talent to light up the world. Every good example people will follow. Agree?

154. *"When I stand before God at the end of my life, I would hope that I would not have a single bit of talent left and could say:" I used everything you give me."* Erma Bombeck

Talent is like every other lasting battery with predicted life span to be used in time all. Agree?

155. *"If you are young and Talented, it is like you have wings."* Haruki Murakami

Talent is greatest power that everyone may feel like has wings. It is great power for those that are able to discover and use it. Agree?

156. *"The difference between a successful person and others, is not lack of strength, not a lack of knowledge, but rather lack of will."* Vince Lombardi

Talent is skill and will is energy that moves action forward. Agree

157. *Talent is life direction where opportunity is hard work."* Dragan

For every hard working Talented person opportunity opens its door for all that possess power to wait. Patience is also power that never fails. Agree?

158. *"The true meaning of life is to plant trees, under whose shade you do not expect to sit."*

Nelson Henderson.

Talent abides in benevolent heart that loves entire world. Agree?.

159. *"Opportunities are usually disguised as a hard work, so most people don't recognize them."*

Ann Landers.

It is hard work that rejects people from opportunity that has been frequently presented to many people. Agree?

160. *"Our opportunities to do good are our talent.""* Cotton Mather

Main purpose for every Talent is to do good for others. That what Talent is for and why we are publishing for everyone to have it and to do good work for many. Agree?

161. *"The secret of success in life is for man to be ready for his opportunity when it comes."*

Benjamin Disraeli.

That is life of every Talented person to work hard and to wait for opportunity. Being patience is being ready for success. That is in general condition that everyone must accepted. Agree?

162. *"I have not failed. I have found 10,000 ways that won't work."* Thomas Edison.

Talented man is man that persevere until right time comes. Talented man woks hard and gain necessary life experience. He grows and his Talent mature with every fail.

163. *"We can left circumstances rule us, or we can take charge and rue our lives from within."*

Earl Nightingale

We have given power that is within us to resist all challenges and to control destiny of our lives. Agree?

164. *"Stand up to your obstacles and do something about them. You will find that they haven't half the strength you think they have,"* Norman Vincent Peale.

You are not without help, you are not without power. You are armed well within which is in your heart your given power your power of love your Talent. Talent always encourage. That what talent is for. Agree?

165. *"He who knows other is wise. He who knows himself is enlightened."* Lao Tzu

It is purpose of this small book that everyone knows about himself, about his given gift his

Talent as a life as a life purpose as a life direction as one the best friend that you may have, to light up your life. Agree?

166. *"Create the legacy of a better world. Leave this world a better place that you found it."*

Jonathan Lockwood Huie

You have your Talent do it the best you can according to the power of your given Talent. Agree?

167. *"You gain strength, courage, and confidence by every experience in which you really stop to look fear in the face. You must do things which you think you cannot do."* Eleanor Roosevelt.

With every experience you gain not only strength but also being more courageous because courage is growing while going through storms. Agree?

Be courageous and may your heart be strong. All you who are waiting for Lord. Prov. Agree?

168. *"Live a life of Bold and Courageous Action inspired by Powerful Dreams"* Jonathan Lockwood Huie

Powerful Talent always Dreams Powerful Dreams that are Ready for Powerful Action. Agree?

169. *"To live is to choose. But to choose well, you must know who you are and what you stand for, where you want to go and why you want to get there. S. Jobs*

When you chose your Talent which is when you discover who you are born to be and to become your life, your life direction and your life goal you are standing on solid ground for good. Agree?

170. *"To accomplish great things, we must not only act, but also dream; not only plan but also believe."*

Anatole France

We all dream but we also must believe in our dreams in order to decide to act. Believing in self in your

Talent is power to move you forward in action. Agree?

171. *"One does not discover new land without consenting to lose sight of the shore for a very long time."* Andre Gide

Life of discovery is journey into new and unknown land leaving everything behind without ever turning back for that is only discovery as process always moving forward. Agree?

172. *"He who believes is strong; he who doubts is weak. Strong conviction precede great action."*

Louisa Nay Alcott.

If you do believe in your Talent you will use it, you will move forward and you will gain strength with ever move forward, toward happiness that is always waiting on the end of your life path. Agree?

173. *"Failure is success if we learn from it."* Malcolm Forbes.

Every failure is new experience that has magic power to move you forward toward your successful life

Agree?

174. *"Winners Never Quit, and Quitters Never Win."* Vince Lombardi.

In every Talent there is no in vocabulary word quitting. It is only word forward. Agree?

175. *"Start by doing what is necessary; then do what is possible; and suddenly you are doing impossible."* St. Francis of Assisi

Slowly, gradually and carefully is talent's way doing things one at the time with one step at the time.

Each brick creating solid foundation to the next one. Agree?

176. *"Believe that life is worth living and your belief will help creating facts."* William James.

Believe in your talent because your Talent is you life which is worth living and never regretting. Agree?

177. *"Nothing in life is to be feared, it is only to be understood. Now is the time to understand more, so that we may fear less.""* Marie Curie.

It is Talent to be understood and to be accepted, which will bring great understanding without any fear, as a beneficial and protective power. Agree?

178. *"Success does not come to you, you go to it."* Mara Collins

Success follows every act of hard work and endurance guided by the power of your talent. Agree?

Practice #3

301. *"Believe in yourself. Have a faith in your abilities. Without a humble but reasonable confidence in your own powers you cannot be successful or happy."* Norman Vincent Peale.

Everyone who knows its own power and trust in its own power in its given free gift its Talent must be confident on a way to his success and happiness what every talent guaranty." Agree

302. *"Most people give up just when they are about to achieve success. They quit in the one yard line.*

They give up at the last minute of the game one foot from a winning touchdown." Ross Perot

It is your power, your Talent that never give up to the end of proposed plan. That is real power of Hope that is even more then hope but faith in self's power. Agree?

303. *"It is our choice... that show what we truly are, far more than our abilities."* J.K. Rowing

It is not only our abilities but something even more powerful that is close related to our ability our inner power, our Talent. Agree?

304. *"Don't let one cloud obliterate the whole sky"* Anais Nin

There is in every life many small obstacles as they call clouds that will block whole sky which is our universal power our Talent our life and our life purpose." Agree?

305. *"Life must be lived and curiosity kept alive. One must never, for whatever reason, turn his back on life."* Eleanor Roosevelt.

Our Talent is given as our life that must be lived to fulfill given purpose. Remember Emma Bombeck

306. *"Everyone has their own talents. It's up to the individual to see what you can actually do"*

Win Butler.

Talent is free gift but personal great responsibilities what to do with it.

Agree?

307. *"The greatest evil which fortune can inflict on men is to endow them with small talent and great ambitions."* Marquis de Vauvenargues

It could be mistake of the nature or some mental disturbance resulted from the surrounding environment. From history we may see examples of some world leaders that injected so many misery involving entire humanity. Agree?

308. *Changes always comes bearing gifts."* Price Pritchett

If you change, if you grow then your Talent changes as become more mature able to bear many new good fruits. Every change means personal progress and new results. Agree?

309. *"Great works are performed not by strength but by perseverance."* Samuel Johnson

We may possess everything but missing only one thing like perseverance then all other parts become helpless. We must be complete person in order for perfect functions. Agree?

310. *"Those who believe they can do something and those who believe they can't are both right."*

Henry Ford.

Believing in self is confidence as personal power as a part of personal abilities to look every challenge straight in the eyes without being hesitant. Agree?

311. *"You can't do anything about length of your life, but you can do something about its width and depth."* Evan Esar.

It is Talent that brings meaning of our life to be worthy of living and even happiness that comes with Talents power we may expect better health and even length of our life. Talent is our real power. Agree?

312. *"Existence needs you. Without you, something will be missing in existence and nobody can replace it. That's what gives you dignity that the whole existence will miss you."* Osho

For those that walk through their life without active talent is nothing but being missing by whole existence. It simple means that entire world will be missing you and not only you but all those that are not for some reason able to have that precious Spiritual gift for real life. Everyone will be miss because everyone is counted. Agree?

313. *"The influence you exert is through your own life, and what you've become yourself."*

Eleanor Roosevelt

You have been torn to be something and to become someone in order to present yourself in your life to this world as one to be and to become positive influence. Agree?

314. *"Where there is a will there is a way."* Old English proverb.

Talent without will power is no talent. Agree?

315. *"If you wait to do everything until you're sure it's right you'll probably never do much of anything."* Win Borden

No open door of opportunity will guaranty that everything will be right. You must be ready for every occasion and to never pas any opportunity because you never be certain about qualities of that sudden opportunity. Agree?

316. *"There are risk and cost to action. But they are far less than the long range risk of comfortable inaction.* John F. Kennedy

For that simple reason every talent is given for one purpose which is action that should never be replace for inaction. Because with inaction you will never able to find out what would be result of action.

Agree?

317. *"The greater the obstacle, the more glory in overcome it"* Moliere

That all depend on the power of given Talent and difficulties that obstacle to be faced. More power more difficulties and more glory. With less power less difficulties and less glory. Agree?

318. *"Nature does not hurry, but everything is accomplished."* Lao Tzu

Look in the nature and learn that every process is going its slow pace but steady pace without hesitation. You must observe that pace that comes from one small seed to the large tree to bring many fruits for all and to never brag about that. What is the even more interesting that no one is going to take credit about that good beneficial work. Natural way of being patience. Agree?

319. *"Do not let what you cannot do interfere with what you can do."* John Wooden

That so important message for everybody to comprehend its power and keep it in its personal limit.

Unless someone more ambitious intend to challenge personal power and to go from something that is possible to the level of impossible to lean about its own limit or even to make some improvement.

Agree?

320. *"A man who is master of patience is master of everything else."* George Savile.

Every talent has its own pace its own rhythms to be follow patiently in order to prevent any discrepancy between you and your talent. Pace yourself and do not worry about end result which will come well naturally. Agree?

321 *"If you are not in the moment, you are either looking forward to uncertainty, or back to pain and regret."* Jim Carrey

Your Talent works only when you are in the moment, in time when you act and in same time your talent acts with you. Agree?

322. *"If you are depressed you are living in the past. If you are anxious you are living in the future.*

If you are at peace you are living in the present." Lao Tzu.

Your Talent is not living in past neither in future. Your talent is a peace in the present time. Agree?

323. *"Do not dwell in the past, do not dream of the future, concentrate the mind on the present moment."* The Buddha

It is time when you are most effective and time when your Talent is ONLY with you. Agree?

324. *"Once you make decision, the Universe conspire to make it happen."* Ralph Waldo Emerson.

Your Talent is universal because it is given to every living soul to do good for entire humanity. Talent is from universe and also when work has been done goes back to universe. Agree?

325. *"Go confidently in the direction of your dreams. Live life you have imagined."* Henry David Thoreau

Keep dreaming and let you Talent do the works of your dreams. That what talent is for. Agree

326. *"You are never too old to set another goal or to dream a new dreams."*
C.S. Lewis

You are getting old but your Talent is always same; young and ready for action. Use it all the time.

We grow and get old but talent only mature and biome more effective.

Agree?

327. *"Coming together is beginning. Keeping together is progress. Working together is success."*

Henry Ford.

United Talents create progress as a benefit for all. Talent's way. Agree?

328. *"Team work is the ability to work together toward common vision, as a power that allows common people to attain uncommon objectives."* Carnegie

In unity is the strength in family in society and in entire humanity to realize common good for common people. Agree?

329. *"Teamwork is so important that it is virtually impossible for you to reach the height of your abilities."* Brian Tracy

Working together talents are able to enhance each other creating not two and two are four but five.

Working together everybody gain in strength and result is lot better than individual work. That is law of the nature which every talent follows Agree?

330. *"You do not get harmony when everybody sings same song."* Doug Floyd

Different Talents and different sound and one beautiful music. Combination of different talents working together always brings success. Agree?

331. *"The habit of persistence is the habit of victory."* Herbert Kaufman.

Talent is the skill that is working and enduring duo to personal inborn ability persistence. We simple in our life to be victorious need more than anything is persistence. Agree?.

332. *"One who gains strength by overcoming obstacles possesses the only strength which can overcome adversity."* Albert Schweitzer

By persistence we conquer obstacles in same time we gain in strength for further action. Agree?

333. *"To climb steep hills requires a slow pace at first."* William Shakespeare

For every hard and challenging prospect we must take slow in the beginning to build first solid foundation and then slowly increase activities. Agree?

334. *"A journey of a thousand miles begins with a single step."* Lao Tzu

Well established wisdom from centuries is that everything must be slow in the beginning to establish good position before things start moving with increased speed." Agree?

335. *"Our greatest weakness lies in giving up. The most certain way to succeed is always to try just one more time."* Thomas Edison

One things is true that talent never gives up. We with our weak ability do that. Trying again is always welcome from our power, from our helper, our Talent. Agree?

336. *"Adversity has the effect of eliciting talents, which in prosperous circumstances would have lain dormant."* Horace

We need stormy weather to awake our Talent who has tendency in peaceful circumstance to fall in sleep. Talent always keeps looking for opportunity which is for every talent invitation for action.

Like everything in our lives we all need something to incite our sleepy talent for actions. Agree?

Agree?

337. "It is our choice... that show what we truly are, far more than our abilities." Albert Einstein

Our choices are what we are and we are what our Talent is. Ability is only our energy our ability to carry our Talents work. Agree?

338. "Any human anywhere will blossom in a hundred unexpected Talents and capacity simple by being given the opportunity to do so." Doris Lessing

It is the door that opens to let power comes out and not before. Open door is opportunity for every waiting Talent ready for action. Many people in spite having Talents keep their doors close for the simple reason to keep peace and not to be disturb. They live closed life far from every life action and every opportunity for their given power as it is in most cases for luck of courage. Agree?

339. "Like a kick in the butt, the forces of event wakes slumberous Talents." Edward Hoagland

That kick must be strong enough to open the door for slumbered talent to get out for action. Agree?

340. "You will never do anything in this world without courage. It is the greatest quality of the mind next to honor." Aristotle.

Courage is virtue comes as a habit by doing things from small to greater one in order to become a great power to carry every skill-Talented person from one to next action without fear. For that fearless condition we may deserved honor. Agree?

341. "You are what you do and not what you say I will do." Mohandas Gandhi

You are doing what your Talent is what makes you what your Talent is. Agree?

342. "We don't see things as they are, we see things as we are." Anais Nin

Eyes of your heart your spiritual eyes as expression who you are and all related to your given Talent. We may call it intuition. It is power of heart power of feelings. Agree

343. *"Faith plus action becomes unstoppable."* Jonathan Lockwood Huie

You must trust your Talent your life and life direction to take you successfully toward your predicted goal.

344. *"When I do good, I feel good. When I do bad, I feel bad."* Abraham Lincoln.

Use your talent to do good and to feel good for your talent to become your religion your secular religion. as a power to grow from secular to humanistic religion and latter even to universal religion as our talent mature to the highest level, where he A. Lincoln stands. Agree?

345. *"In the arena of human life, the honor and reward fall to those who show their good qualities in action."* Aristotle.

Use your talent and act and your action will bring you honor reward and real happiness on end of your life path. Agree?

346. *"The only place where your dream becomes impossible is in your own thinking."* Robert H. Schuller

This words must be always remembered well because when ever comes doubt about some intention to be taken with great deal of skepticism we must know that origin is not external but it is in our own soul. Talent is one that must be savior in every critical situation. Agree?

347. *"All our dreams can come true, if we have the courage to pursue them."* Walt Disney

Where there is doubt there is no courage. Then you must do something to develop power of being courageous. That needs time and that needs dedication to succeed. Agree?

348. *"The greatest mistake you can make in life is to be continually fearing you will make one."*

Elbert Hubbard

Take you Talent and go slowly step by step and believe that there is no mistake but only experience.

Every mistake is new knowledge new experience where direction you should not go again.

Avoid that mistaken road to take again. Agree?

349. *"Always be a first-rate version of yourself, instead of second rate-version of somebody else."*

Judy Garland

By who your Talent is, that is you, that is your life, that is your live purpose, that is your life direction, that is everything that you possess in your life, that will take you to the happy end.

Agree?

350. *"Life is either a daring adventure or nothing."* Helen Keller

That is your own decision which way from those two you will take as you life way. Take your Talent you will have his direction to be your daring adventure rather than nothing. Agree?

351. *"Don't die with your music still inside you. Listen to your intuitive inner voice and find what passion steers your soul."* Wayne Dyer

Listen to your heart where your Talent is and follow, Talent is your passion that guides your life.

Do not die before all your talent's power has been used. Remember Bombeck. Agree?

352. *"A ship in harbor is safe- but that is not what ships are for."* John A Shedd

Let your ship frilly sail in the direction of your Talent as your life way. Agree?

353. *"We must become the changes we wish to see in the world."* Mohandas Gandhi

Your world must become your world your purpose in the life. With your Talent and your purpose you will influence desired changes in your world. Be a leader, be innovator and make yourself, and your work part of your world changes. When you work hard your experience changes and in same time you change the world. Agree?

354. *"I am one with the power and wisdom of the Universe. I have all that I need."* Louise L. Hay

You have your Talent you have all. Talent is from the Universe. Agree?

355. *"Every day in every way I am getting better and better."* Anonymous

That what happens when you follow your given Power your Talent. Agree?

356. *"Standing in the inspiring vision of my future, I boldly take every step-large and small with courage and intent."* Jonathan Lockwood Huie

Your Talent is your future to take you boldly forward according to your own decision.. Agree?

357. *"There is beauty and achievement in the common place for those with eyes to see beyond."*

Jonathan Lockwood Huie

Talent leads you to see things that many cannot. It is as seeing miracle in common. Agree?

358 *"Simple living is the way to happy living."* Jonathan Lockwood Huie

Life with you Talent is both. Simple and happy. Agree?

359. *"It is ok to make mistake. Mistakes are our teachers-they help us to learn.""* John Bradshaw

That Talents way-learning way where every mistake is new learning. Agree?

360. *"Endurance is not just the ability to bear a hard thing but to turn it into glory."* William Barclay

Every Talent needs endurance to turn things into glory. Endurance is open door to the glory. Agree?

361. *"Not in achievement, but in endurance of the human soul, does it show its divine grander and its alliance with infinitive."*

Only with your Talent that is divine power what makes it infinitive. Agree?

362. *"This is no time for easy and comfort. It is time to dare and endure."* Winston Churchill

It was true in his time but is also true in our time. To dare and endure as a privilege of Talented one's

363. *"A hero is an ordinary individual who finds the strength to persevere and endure in spite of overwhelming obstacles."* Christopher Reeve

Everyone has its own talent but talent to act require challenges as obstacles to be overcome in order to be by some call hero. Talent and challenges are what make man hero. Agree?

364. *"I will love the light for it shows me the way, yet I will endure darkness because it shows me stars."* Og Mandino.

Life with Talent is life in light but when darkness comes it always has the way to the light back, while seeing stars is sign that light is coming slowly in time when not everything is dark.

That is trust, that is the faith in Talent that will always help especially in time of darkness. Agree?

365. *"As we work to create light for others, we naturally light our own way."* Mar Anne Radmacher

That is Talents way to help others to bring light to others working hard for others what light up his own way. Agree?

366. *"Trust in the light. Darkness is not a force-it is merely the absence of light."* Jonathan Lockwood Huie

Trust in your talent and whenever you see darkness work for the light. That is different between right and wrong, where light is right and darkness is wrong. Light will bring light in darkness but not otherwise Agree?

367. *"All the darkness of the world cannot extinguish the light of a single candle, yet one candle can illuminate all the darkness."* Jewish Hanukah Prayer

Power of your talent is power of love, power of light, able to light up entire world. Agree?

368. *"Beyond a doubt, truth bears the same relation to falsehood as a light to darkness.""*

Leonardo de Vinci

You talent is light and truth always abides in light and never in darkness where falsehood lives.

Agree?

369. *"So powerful is the light of unity that it can illuminate the whole earth,"* Baha'u'llah

United Talented people will bring light-prosperity to whole earth. Unity is power per say. Agree?

Repeated aphorism

370. *"Do what you feel in your heart to be right. You will be criticized anyway."* Eleanor Roosevelt

Be steadfast in your faith. Trust your Talent your life way. That is right way. Agree?

371. *"As for accomplishment, I just did what I had to do as thins come along."* Eleanor Roosevelt

As for every ready Talent opportunity keep comings one after other to be completed. Many do keep missing their opportunities but Talent is ready for any one that comes along. Agree?

372. *"A thankful heart is not only the greatest virtue, but the parent of all the virtue."* Cicero

Talent is the power of love and love is parent of all virtue. There is no courage without love. There is no justice without love. There is no good temper without love. All prudency is founded on Love

Love is everything in same way as talent is. Agree?

373. *"Remember that the happiest people are not those getting more, but those giving more."*

H. Jackson Brown Jr.

If you live with your Talent you will be living happy life because Talent is giving and not taking.

Agree?.

374. *"Far away there in the sunshine are my highest aspirations. I may not reach them, but I can look up and see their beauty, believe in them, and try to follow where they lead."* Louise May Alcott

Talent is our light and our aspiration to follow in our life believing in its beauty that brings light to this world. Agree?

375. *"The miracle is not that we do this work, but that we are happy to do it."* Mother Teresa

We must accept fact that every work of the Talent is nothing but happy experience. Agree?

376. *"Life is succession of lessons which we must be lived to be understood."* Helen Keller

Talent breaths from one lesson to other as a everyone life lesson to become another brick in its building house. Every lesson becomes new personal property from that activities. Agree?

377. *"Whatever you can do, or dream you can. Begin it. Boldness has genius, power and magic in it.*

Begin it now," Johann Wolfgang von Goethe

You have your Talent then keep dreaming as every Talent dose and start doing what your dream is.

Be bold and make your dream reality as a main purpose of your life. Agree?

378. *"Our lives means exactly what we say they mean- no more, no less. Each of us chooses their path in life."* Jonathan Lockwood Hue

Path in your life is your Talent what presents you life meaning.

379. *"Never worry about action but only inaction."* Winston Churchill

Your Talent's life is life of action and be sure that it must be involve in very active opportunity.

Always keep looking for opportunity because the door usually opens and close quickly. Do not miss.

Agree?

380. *"Never give up, for that is just the place and the time that the tide will turn."*

Harriet Beecher Stowe

Keep attentive for every opportunity. Always keep in mind that Talent is activity (and never) inactivity that never stops before real end of achievement comes. Agree?

381. *"If you can imagine it, you can achieve it. If you can dream it, you can become it."*

William Arthur Ward

Everything that you imagine your Talent will be able to achieve. You keep dreaming and let your

Talent keep working. There is close relation between your dreams and the power of your Talent.

If you dream more than your talent can achieve that is not dreaming but only fantasy. Agree?

382. *"Don't Limit Your Challenges. Challenge your Limit."* Anonymous.

It is progress one step at the time, going slowly and surely. By experience you must know your limit and then one step at the time to establish every step solidly before take next one. Agree?

383. *"A little more persistence, a little more effort, and what seemed hopeless failure may turn to the glorious success."* Elbert Hubbard

Follow your heart and never think about mistake. There is no mistake but only learning experience

Agree?

384. *"Success demands singleness of purpose."* Vince Lombardy

As every program must have its purpose your talent will take you that way because your Talent is your purpose." Agree?

385. *"Confidence is contagious. So is lack of confidence."* Vince Lombardi

So for every team it is so important that we have all players filled with optimism and confidence because even one decayed apple may contaminate rest of the company. Agree?

386. *"Never let the fear of striking out get in your way."* Babe Ruth

Fear is great opponent of every Talent on a way of creating positive result. It is like virus in computer. Agree?

387. *"Mind or heart are like parachutes. They only function when they are open."* James Dewar.

For all they did discover their given gift their given Talent have open heart and ready Talent for every requested action. That is the difference between Talented and those that never open their heart. Agree?.

388. *"Do you want to know who you are? Don't ask. Act! Action will delineate and define you."* Thomas Jefferson.

By acting you will learn that hose activities that you do love is activities from your given heart where your Talent is what makes you who you are. Loving what you do is your Talent and Talent is your life which is who you are. Agree?

389. *"Never give up, for that is just the place and the time the tide will turn."* Harriet Beecher Stowe

Persistency is the part of optimism to persist until succeed. Never give up because you will never know where is the right time. Agree?

390. *"Thinking will not overcome fear but action will."* W. Clement Stone

That is proper medicine for fear that may block every activities for your given power your Talent, where activity is antidote for fear

Agree?

391. *"Action is a great restorer and builder of confidence. Inaction is not only the result but he cause of fear."* Norman Vincent Peale.

You have your Talent let him go free in action that will subdue every fear.

Talent is the freedom from fear. Agree?

392. *"No one can find inner peace except by working, not in self-centered way, but for the whole human family."* Peace Pilgrim.

It is clearly Talent's way that never works for self but for many others. For the real talented power that never turns attention to self but always for the goodness for all. Agree?

393. *"You can't live a perfect day without doing something for someone who will never be able to repay back."* John Wooden.

It is power of love which is in your heart where your Talent abide. Your talent is the power of love for doing good for others and not for self. Agree?

394. *"Nothing is impossible to a willing heart."* John Keywood

It is your heart where your power is where your Talent abides willing to act for every opportunity.

Talent makes everything possible according to its power. Not every Talent is the same and with same power. Agree.?

395. *"The way is not in the sky. The way is in the heart."* The Buddha

It is your Talent that is in your heart. Talent is your life. Talent your life purpose. Talent is your life direction. Talent is your way to your happiness. Agree?

396. *"Only from the heart can you touch the sky."* Rumi

Only through your Talent and loving care for others you become part of universe because

Talent is from universe. Agree?

397. *"Something the heart sees what is invisible to the eye."* H. Jackson Brown. Jr.

It is the feelings, it is the intuition it is talent to anticipate to foresight things even before eyes sees it. Agree?

389. *"Trust your own inner guidance. Have faith that your steps are carrying you toward your dreams. Keep your eyes on the heavens and believe that your feet carry you well."* Jonathan Lockwood Huie

Trust your leader your Talent believe that whole universe is with you and that your feet are solidly fixed to the ground to be not taken away from your right direction. Agree?

399. *"Your mind knows only some things. Your inner voice, your instinct, knows everything. If you listen to what you know instinctively, it will always lead you down to the right path."*

Henry Winkler.

Talent is your own guide on your own pathway. Talent is like fingerprints, which endures everything and cannot be changed in anything else, but only to be nurtured and made it perfect

Listen to him it is your instinct or better to say natural voice. Agree?

400. "To know even one life has breathed easier because you have lived. That is to have succeeded." Ralph Waldo Emerson.

That is life opportunity and only opportunity that your precious gift your Talent can bring to your life.

Agree?

401. *"If we have no peace, it is because we have forgotten that we belongs to each others."* Mother Teresa

Talents must live and work together by being complementary to each others because they are all different in same way human organs are different being united working to help and support each others creating strong and healthy body. Agree?

Practice #4

401. *"Talent is cheaper than table salt. What separates talented individual from the successful one is a lot of hard work."* Stephen King

Talent without hard work is worth as table salt. Agree?

2. *"Hope is a talent like any other."* Storm Jameson

It is the faith that you hope what makes you Talented one. Faith in your talent is your hope. Agree?

3. *"I would like to be remembered as someone who did the best she could with the talent she had."* J.K. Rowling.

She had power with limitation and used all what she had. Nothing more and nothing less. Agree?

4. *"I really believe that everyone has a talent, ability, or skill that he can mine to support himself and to succeed in life."* Dean Koontz

Talent is the skill and ability is compliment to talent to succeed. Agree?

5. *"Take pride in exactly what it is you do and remember it's ok to fail as long as you don't give up."* Dan O'Brien

When you do your talent work never ever give up whatever may take place because

Talent never loses its power to the end of its destination. Agree?

6. *"Humankind has not woven the web of life. We are but one thread within it.*

Whatever we do to the web, we do ourselves. All things are bound together.

All things connect." Chief Seattle

As a talented one we are never alone and whatever we do good or not we are doing not only for self but entire web. All you may call it entire humanity. We are all One.

7. *"You are always a student, never a master. You have to keep moving forward."* Conrad Hall

You grow but your talent keep maturing and getting better and better to reach its potential as long as power is in action before battery become empty. That is end of its power and you are without help any more. Agree?

8. *"Everybody has talent, it's just a matter of moving around until you've discover. what it is."* George Lucas

I would just use looking instead moving. Or better to say keep moving and looking

Agree?

9. *"That is the goal. Just to go and to try to prove anybody wrong but just let your talent speak for themselves."* Robert Griffin III

Your talent is your life direction for you to only follow it without any competitions.

Agree?

10. *"Our opportunity to do good are our talents."* Cotton Matter.

Talent is our life purpose and what is doing good it is good to all. Agree?

11. *"Motivation will almost always beat mere talent."* Norman Ralph Augustine

Some believe that motivation is talent but we must take that motivation is only humans ability to sustain all possible difficulties and is only servant and supporter for every talented work. It is being motivated but what not affect your skill what your talent is. Agree?

12. *"Nothing can stop the (person) with the right mental attitude from achieving (their) goal."* Thomas Edison

Every talented one is motivated to succeed base on positive and optimistic mental attitude. Agree?

13. *"Let me tell you the secret that has led me to my goal. My strength lies solely in my tenacity."* Louis Pasteur

Talent was his life direction but his strength was in strength to continue in every case or to be persistent in order to persevere all possible difficulties. Some may call it being stubborn. Agree?

14. *"What lies behind us and what lies before us are tiny matter compared to what lies within us."* Ralph Waldo Emerson

Everything is what we are and what our abilities are There are so many things but all are with same purpose to support activities of our talent. Endurance, persevere, strength, tenacity. motivation, attitude. longing and many, many others effective attributes. Agree?

15. *"Our lives are define not by the challenges we encounter, but by how we respond to those challenges."* Jonathan Lockwood Huie

It all about our powerful abilities that is able to respond by all those personal attributes one possess. Agree?

16. *"If we say, "That is never going to work." then chance are excellent it never will."*

John Assaraf.

That must be not expression of one optimist but one who is strongly pessimist.

Agree?

17. *"In spite of unseasonable wind, snow and unexpected weather of all sorts-a gardener still plants. And tends what they have planted believing that spring will come."* Mary Anne Radmacher.

It is natural optimism because that is fight for life; fight for survival that is only possible by the power of humans abilities and directed by their given Talent to do things right for self and others Agree?

18. *"Optimism is the faith that leads to achievement. Nothing can be done without hope or confidence." Helen Keller*

Those that possess active talent are those that have a faith in their power what makes then confident to achieve their given goal.

That all presents clear difference between optimist and pessimist. Agree?

19. *"First. Be brave, dream big, and chase your dreams. You will have your failures, but you will grow from every honest effort."* Bill Clinton

He was brave and dream bid dream and succeed because he was optimist trusted in his own talent. Agree?

2o.*" Don't Limit Your Challenges... Challenge Your Limits.* "Anonymous

If you possess both-your abilities and your powerful talent then go and do challenge your limits. Agree?

21. *"At all time and under all circumstances we have the power to transform the qualities of our lives."* Werner Erhard.

Again your power is in our abilities and our talent our life direction and our life opportunities. Agree?

22. *"It is your time-it is your life- You get to choose how to use it.".*"

Jonathan Lockwood Huie

It is your talent, it is your life way, follow it. Agree?

23. *"Educating the mind without educating the heart is no education at all."* Aristotle.

Depending only upon your mind in education without educating your heart where the power of love your talent abides is the less than half a man. Agree?

24. *"A good head and good heart are always a formidable combination.*

Nelson Mandela

We need to educated both. Our head-mind and our heart-talent to become complete one ready for formidable display-being impressive as hard worker. Agree?

25. *"To me education is a leading out what is already there in the pupils soul."*

Muriel Spark

It is in the heart it is your talent that needs to be educated

26. *"The greatest gift is a portion of thyself."* Ralph Waldo Emerson

Only worthiest gift that is in yourselves is your power of love in your heart your talent

Agree?

27. *"If there is anything that a man can do well, I say let him do it. Give him a chance"*

Abraham Lincoln

Everyone needs opportunity to show who that one is and what one can do it. Agree?.

28. *"We make a living by what we get. We make a life by what we give."*

Winston Churchill

We get our gift and we give its given power to the world. Agree?

29. *"When we do the best that we can, we never know What miracle is wrought in our life, or in the life of another."* Helen Keller.

Work of every talent is work of miracle for self and others. But more for others and not much or nothing for self. Agree?

30. *"No individual has any right to come into the world and go out of it without leaving something behind."* George Washington Craver

Everyone who has his talent discovered, educated and devoted to the life for others' to never leave this world without any foot prints. Agree?

31. *"The only gift is a portion of thyself."* Ralph Waldo Emerson.

Only gift that you give others is from your heart where power of love your talent abides. Talent works hard not for self but always for other. What real talent does.

Agree?

32. *The more we care for the happiness of others, the greater is our own sense of well-being."* Tenzin Gyatso

Every work talent accomplish brings on end happiness for all. That is talent's way.

Agree?

33. *"Great opportunities to help others seldom come, but small ones surround us every day,"* Sally Koch

That calls for every talent to be much attentive for all those small opportunities which are daily phenomenon with chance to become benefits for many. Agree?

34. *"Give the world the best you have and it may never be enough. Give the world your best anyway."* Mother Teresa

You can give your best as your talent is the best. Different people different talents and different power which is all according to persons abilities. Gift must be measure by the gifts power. Agree?

35. *"The miracle is not that we do this work, but that we are happy to do it."*

Mother Teresa

It is not about happiness but it is about love that have for what we are doing. That is what talent is and that is love of doing thing according to given talent. Agree?

36. *"Look well into thyself, there is a source of strength which will always spring up if thou will always look there." Marcus Aurelius*

Every man is adorned with many different strength as personal gift his talent as his abilities that are so many that will show themselves if you do look carefully. Keep look in and let us know what you see.? is it your will power, or your endurance or your perseverance or any other of many that are living as a part of your soul and waiting. Agree?

37. *"Life is not about waiting for the storm to pass. It is about learning how to dance in the rain." Vivian Greene*

It is our talent that is most effective in stormy days. We use talent and with every use talent become better and stronger in same way as our muscle does with exercise. Agree?

38. *It is better to light up a candle than the curse the darkness." Chinese proverbs*

Your talent brings light in time of difficulties where talent is light and difficult time is darkness. In time of darkness use your talent to light up the world. Agree?

439. *"You are never too old to set another goal or to dream new dream." C.S.* Lewis

You grow and get old but your talent only mature and never get old. Talent is not earthly, talent is not fleshly, talent is universal that belongs to every living soul.

Agree?

440. *"Life is not easy for any of us. But what is that? We must have perseverance and above all confidence in ourselves." Marie Curie*

Our talent is our skill that performs all things even difficult one's to conquer with will power and perseverance as a main talent's supporter. Agree?

441. *"The key to happiness is having dreams. The key to success is making your dream come true." Anonymous*

You keep dreaming and let your talent do the work of your dream what brings success and happiness. Agree?

442. *"And in the end, it's not the years in your life that counts, it's the life in your years."* Abraham Lincoln

It's all about your talent your gift your free gift what did you do with it. Agree?

443. *"Few are the giants of the soul that actually feel that the human race is their family circle." Freya Stark*

Every talented one is the giant that belongs rightfully to the human's circle. We are all one.

444. *"The reason why the world lacks unity, and lies broken in heaps, is because man is disunited with himself."* Ralph Waldo Emerson.

United man is one who is living and acting united with its given power it's given free gift its talent together with its powerful inborn abilities. That is united and completed man to act as it is expected for one that is walking in its life in right direction together in unity with others talents. Agree?

445. *"Individually, we are one drop. Together, we are an ocean." Ryunosuke Satoro*

Unity is power that enlarge the world and carry progress. Agree?

446. *"I am a poor man and of little worth who is laboring in that art that God has give me in order to extend my life as long as possible. Michelangelo*

Talent is greatest power that work as long as power of that free gift last. Talent never quits. Life for talented one stops only when power of given talent expire.

Agree?

447. *"Curiosity keeps one young-in thought and action.""* Jonathan Lockwood Huie

Every talent is curious in thoughts and in action as a way to salvation. Remember great Michelangelo who keeps working in order to live longer as it is a case for every talented man who is in action to the last breath. Agree?

448. *"Too many people grow up. That's the real trouble with the world, too many people grow up. They forget."* Walt Disney

In same time they grow up and forget. They forget something? Eventually they died and forget to do something. what? Agree?

449. *"Don't go through life-grow through life."* Eric Butterworth

You grow but your talent mature through active life what we call being better or being more experienced. You grow and your talent acts. Acting one mature.

Agree?

450. *"Faith is taking the first step even when you don't see the whole staircase."*

Martin Luther King Jr.

Way the talent works in discovery through land of darkness and unknown where with every step brings more and more light which talent is to bring light in the darkness of our world. On end of its pathway everything is in light and there is no more darkness. That is work of talent that is way of human's progress. Agree.?

451. *"Change is the law of life. And those that look only to the past or present are certain to miss the future."* John F. Kennedy.

Talent dreams looking forward and follows its dream in action. Agree?

452. *"I do not want to die... until I have faithfully made the most of my talent and cultivate the seed that was placed in me until the small twig has grown."*

Kathe Kollwitz

That is your talent your seed to you to grow great tree that will bring many fruits to many. That is your talent your life purpose. Agree?

453. *"From good seed there will be good tree and good fruits. Everything that is in seed as a blue print where entire life way life direction has been printed."*

Every seed is properly prepared to be well adjusted with the power of ability for that person. That all is in order for talent to be able to realize its purpose that are all based upon humans inborn abilities. Agree?

454. *Strength and courage aren't always measured in medals and victories. They are measured in the struggle they overcome. The strongest people aren't always the people who win, they are the people who don't give up when they lose."*

Talent in order to accomplish it given duty needs a lot of endurances and perseverance's to sustain all possible obstacle that are on their way. Agree?

455. *"If you want a place in the sun, you've to put up with few blisters."* Abigail Van Buren

Every hard and enduring work receive pleasant living that is in every case in proportion between level work and level of gratitude. Agree?

456. *"Action without study is fatal. Study without action is futile."*

Mary Ritter Beard.

Every talent needs proper education in order to be able to act sufficiently. However, those that are without talent and go through education never reach the level that is proposed for those that are talented. That is why their action is called futile. Agree?

457. *"When one door of happiness closes, another open, but often we look so long at the closed door that we do not see the one that has been opened for us.*

Helen Keller

Open door is our opportunity that we must not miss and to look constantly very attentive for every opportunity that opens the door to act in time before it closes

Agree?

458. *"Those who believe they can do something, and those who believe they can't are both right."* Henry Ford

That must power or weakness of motivation, which would be how much they are willing to enter in arena of challenging life. Agree?

459. *"Success consist of going from failure to failure without loss of enthusiasm."*

Winston Churchill

Every powerful talent is not breakable by difficulties on a way toward predicted goal well supported by the inborn abilities as one that keeps every action by the power of enthusiasm sustainable from many different obstacles.

460. *"Success is getting what you want, happiness is wanting what you get."*

Dale Carnegie

While you work you are going toward success what you really want. That is your desire to succeed. Happiness is what you expect on the end of your wok as your reward. Agree?

461. *"The difference between a successful person* and *other is not a lack of strength, not a lack of knowledge, but rather a lack of will."* Vince Lombardi

Talent without power of will as a engine that take the talent on the road is of no use"

Talent is only skill that needs power to move forward. Agree?

462. *"Winners never quit and quitters never win."* Vince Lombardi.

That is for you to distinguish between talented on that never quits and non-talented one that always quits. Agree?

463. *"Always be a first version of yourself, instead of a second version of somebody else."* Judi Garland

It is simple. be who your talent is. Agree?

464. *"If your action inspire other to dream more, learn more, do more and become more, you are a leader."* John Quincy Adams

If your life affects others in positive way, that must be the sign that you have talent for being leader. Learn more and continue to lead.

465. *"Confidence is contagious. So is lack of confidence."*

Vince Lombardi

That is also power of your talent to affect other people in positive way. keep it.

Agree?

466. *"Where is great love there are always miracles."* Willa Cather

Love is power that always comes from the heart where power of love our talent abides. Talent is the only sources of great miracles. Agree?

467. *"The greatest gift that you can give to others is the gift of unconditional love and acceptances."* Brian Racy.

Every work from the heart is gift of love as our talent is. Agree?

468. *"Mother is the power of children future because mother is unconditional love."*

Dragan

Mothers loving care helps every child to open its heart and discover it's given gift.

That is how talent is born in loving family. Agree?

469. *"Love is the greatest force for good."* jih

Talent is power of love from heart and is the power for every good deed. Agree?

470. *"You hold onto religion, you know, rules, regulations, traditions. I think what God is interested in is people's heart, and that's hard enough. Bono*

Talent is in the heart and life of talented man is what God is interested the most.

Talent is your gift and that gift is one what makes God interested. And that includes every living soul. Agree?

471. *"Your example is far more influential than any words of instruction, or treats, or even words of encouragement."* Jonathan Lockwood Hue

It is so important in family where parents are like in theatre and children are public for best learning what they will remember lot better than any spoken word. Agree?

472. *"All children are artist. The problem is how to remain an artist once when grow up"* Pablo Picasso.

Every child is born with power of discovery that starts from the first day of their life and imaginative power to act to create all according to its age. Eventually that power of discovery will discover what is in his heart his talent. They need only to be encourage to do what is in its heart. What means to do what they love to do. Agree?

473. *"Anyone willing to be corrected is on its path of life. Anyone refusing has lost his chance."* Proverb.

Every talent going through life is maturing is getting better by learning what we call experience gaining wisdom to learn difference between good and bad. Agree?

474. *"We are all born with a purpose according to our given talent, and we are all entrusted to be able to do that and to do it well according to our abilities."* Dragan.

Every talent that is born in family has to be educated and inborn abilities to be practiced for person to become completed one with educated talent and powerful abilities. Agree?

475. *"We know where most of creativity, the innovation, the stuff that drives productivity lies--in the minds of those closest to the work."* Jack Welch

I would only change from "in the mind" to "in the heart" Agree?

476. *"The purpose of life is not to be happy. The purpose of life is to matter, to be productive, to have it make some difference that you lived at all."*

Happiness always comes on the end of talented life path. Remember that talent is rewarded in universe.

477. *"The journey of a thousand miles must begins with a single step."* Chinese prov.

First step is foundation and also direction for every Talented action. That one decided future of every action. Agree?

478. *"Hope is not a dream, but way of making dreams become reality."*

Cardinal Leon Joseph Suenens.

Hope is quiet and patient while waiting for its time, and loving whatever it does.

Trusting not in time watch but on time that works on a power of wind. Agree?

479. *"Man like nails, lose their usefulness when they lose direction and begin to bend."*

Walter Savage Landor.

Talent is our life direction to be kept without bending but keeping straight. Agree?

480. *"A man is known by his action." Proverb.*

We recognize tree by its fruits. We do not see talent but what we see is the fruits of its action. Agree?

481. *There is no passion to be found playing small-in setting for a life that is less than one you are capable of living." Nelson Mandela.*

You must be well motivated to use your power your talent in full capacity. It is always better to start slow one step at the time until you felt you are ready for full blow. Agree?

482. *"Winning isn't everything, but wanting to win is." Vince Lombardi*

You must be well motivated in order for your talent to work 101% of its capacity

483. *"People often say that motivation doesn't last. Well, neither does bathing-that is why we recommended it daily." Zig Zagler*

Motivation is part of humans ability that like every habits must be practice daily in order to grow to mature and to become one of the best supportive power for every talent's action. Agree?

484. *"You must do the things you think you cannot do." Eleanor Roosevelt.*

They desperately need action and practice of motivation to overcome negative obstructive thoughts. Motivation is preparation for action for every talented one.

485. *"Life isn't about finding yourself. Life is about creating yourself."*

George Bernard Shaw.

Every talent through practice gain experience and mature in wisdom. Agree?

486. *"When in doubt, do it."* Oliver Wendell Holmes.

Have no doubt. Trust in your talent and let him guide you in right direction for you.

Agree?

487. *"Be resolute in your goals, but flexible in your tactics."*

Jonathan Lockwood Huie

When you are resolute you also must be very much motivate to start. What they usually say that every start is difficult that need motivation and rest is only tenacity

Life is full of surprises to really force you to be flexible. Agree?

Agree.?

488. *"Choose rather to be strong of soul than strong of body."* Pythagoras

Your strength is your inner strength and not physical strength. That is great difference between brute strength and strength of your talent your inner strength.

Agree.

489. *"Strength does not come from physical capacity. It comes from an indomitable will."* Mohandas Gandhi

There is no power like will power. Even every talent without will power is worthless.

Agree.?

490. *"Where there is no struggle, there is no strength."* Oprah Winfrey

Every action makes you stronger and stronger. If there is more challenges there is more advancement in strength. Strength like muscles needs constant exercise.

Agree?

491. *"We draw our strength from the very despair in which we have been forced to live."* Cesar Chaves.

It is well known that hard life is one to make you stronger. Hard life hard muscle.

Soft life soft muscle. Every muscle with every level of effort has appropriate respond. Agree?

492. *"There is happiness and inner strength in being your own person."*

Jonathan Lockwood Huie

Be who you are. Be who your talent is. Real power is in your talent your power of love. Agree?

493. *"I gather strength from life's storms."* Jonathan Lockwood Huie

Your way of living will determined your strength, Either in your body or in your soul. Your inner power. Agree?

494. *"Shallow men believe in lack. Strong men believe in cause and effect."*

Ralph Waldo Emerson.

Strength is our confidence and other are looking for soft ball. Agree?

495. *"He who believes is strong, he who doubts is weak."* Louise May Alcott.

Believe in yourself. Believe in your abilities and believe in your talent what will make you strong. Faith is fire that always burns high in time of crisis. Agree?

496. *"Silence is a sources of great strength." Lao Tzu*

Close your mind and take a deep breath to open yourself toward universe where sources of strength abides. Agree?

497. *"He who lives in harmony with himself lives in harmony with the Universe."*

Marcus Aurelius.

When our talent acts in harmony with our abilities we are in same time connected to live in harmony with the universe.

That is our life in harmony with self and with universal power. Agree

498. *"Nothing splendid has ever been achieved except by those who dared believe that something inside of them was superior to circumstances." Bruce Barton*

It is our talent. It is our love. It is our skill that is our inner power to overcome every life presented circumstances before able to achieved our given goal. Agree?

499. *"A coincidence is a small miracles in which God chooses to remain anonymous."*

Anonymous.

It is daily phenomenon that is occurring regularly for all those that are ready to see it and to recognize it and same time to respond properly according to their given talents. Agree?

500. *"If the only prayer you ever say in your entire life is thank you, it will be enough." Meister Eckhart.*

Thank You. Agree?

Practice. #5

All those wise sentences from wise people carry deep meaning as wisdom that resulted on one side from their life experiences in connection with humans wisdom on other side. which is done with good intention for all of as the best instruction for better life for many generations to come.

If everybody write its own opinion we may finely come to most accurate determination to present for continue education and support for all those talented young people for the most prosperous life for them and entire society and even humanity.

1. "To me education as a leading out of what is already there in the pupil's soul."

Muriel Spark

It is all about Humans Talent as a given gift in order to be born as one "to be" something and through proper education "to become" someone according to its given Talent.

Talent without right education is worthless

The question is: is there anything more that Education has responsibility to educate what is a already there in pupil' soul-Talent. Agree?

2. "The artist is nothing without gift, but gift is nothing without work." Emile Zola

Talent is the gift and is enduring hard work. However that must be not all. Must be something else that will work for Talents support? my feeling is: that is longing. Agree?

3. "Artistic Talent is a gift from God and whoever discover it in himself has a certain obligation: to know that he cannot waste this Talent, but must develop it." Pope John Paul

Talent is spiritual gift and wasting that given grace is sin for those that are believers. But for those that are not believers human's Talent has different origin and different responsibility. Agree?

4. *"Often it's not about becoming a new person, but becoming the person you were meant to be, and already are, but don't know how to be."* Heath L. Buckmaster

One that is born with talent that need to be educated properly. Agree?.

5. *"As we let our light shine, we unconsciously give other people permission to do the same."*

M. Williamson

Use your Talent to light up the world. It is power of human's Talent to incite others to the same

Agree?

6. *"Faith is the bird that feels the light and sings when the down is still dark."* *Tagore*

Have a faith in your Talent and let him sing its song. Trusting is power that moves you forward.

Agree?

7. *"The secret of our success is that we never give up."* *Wilma Mankiller*

It is Talent that persevere. No Talent will succeed without perseverance. Agree?

8. *Success is not final, failure is not fatal. It is the courage to continue to counts."*

Winston Churchill

Talent is build upon man's courage. Talent has power to encourage everybody for action, Agree?

9. *"One can never consent to creep when one feels the impulse to soar."* Helen *Keller*

Talent is your wings to take you as high as its power is. Only your Talent can do it. Agree?

10. *"You are what you do, and not what you say you will do,"* Carl Jung

You are what your talent is. Follow your Talent's direction. Agree?

11. *"Courage and perseverance have a magical talisman, before difficulty disappears and obstacles vanish into air."* John Quince Adams

Talent in order to succeed need both. Talent is only personal skill that is build upon personal ability. Those two are only foundation that needs like courage and perseverance and many others supporters. Agree?

12. *"So powerful is light of unity that can illuminate the whole world."* Bah 'U' Lah

Talent's way is life and work in unity with others talents.

13. *"I find the harder I work the more luck I seems to have."* Thomas Jefferson

Talent is enduring hard work."

14. *"If people knew how hard I worked to get my mastery, it would not seem so wonderful at al."* Michelangelo

Talent is enduring hard work. That all depend upon the power of every talent. If talent is powerful than work must be powerful. If talent is heavy than work also must be heavy. Whoever is given more, the more is expected.

15. *"A good head and good heart are always a formidable combination."*

Nelson Mandela

Determination and longing are the best Talent's supporter together with courage and persistence's. Agree?

16. "Talent is wonderful thing, but it won't carry a quitter." Stephen King

Talent needs supporters to be able to fight obstacles and never to give up. Agree?

17. "Achievement seems to be connected with action. Successful man and women keep moving.

They make mistake, but they don't quit." Conrad Clinton

Desire to accomplish they work keep them moving. That is longing that makes man keep going

Agree?

18. "Everyone has talent. What's rare is the courage to follow it to the dark places where it leads." Erica Jung

Talent leads to discovery into dark-unknown places where courage is determined factor toward success. Discovery has purpose to bring light to dark places where fear is main obstacle.

19. "Talent is cheaper than table salt. What separate the talented individual from the successful one is a lot of hard work. "Stephen King

Talent is free gift and great responsibility that require hard work in order to deserve it. Agree?

20. "Be led by your talent, not by your self-loathing; those other things you just have to manage," Russell Brand

Talent is your life direction to be just following. All others like courage, persistence, endurances desire and many other factors are in your hands. Agree?

21. "Your talent determine what you can do. Your motivation determine how much you are willing to do. Your Attitude determine how well you do it." Lou Holtz

Follow your talent and rest is up to you. Agree?

22. "Our talents are the gift that God gives to us... What we make of our talents is our gift back to God." Leo Buscaglia

For those that are believers talent is spiritual gift and must be taken very seriously to do good for One that trusted in you. Agree?

23. "The person born with a talent they are meant to use will find their greatest happiness in using it." Johan Wolfgang von Goethe

Life with your Talent is happy life because every accomplished deed brings on end happiness.

Agree?

24. "There is no such thing as a great talent without great will power." Honoree de Balzac

Talent is direction and will power is engine that moves forward. Agree?

25. "Talent hits a target no one else can hit; genius hits a target no one else can see."

Arthur Schopenhauer

Talent is lie skill one able to do thing what those without talent are not. Genius is able to see like Alexander Fleming in petry dish some yeast call penicilium glaucum to become later salvation for entire world Penicillin. No one before him could see it in same way as no one could see vitamin "C" in Hungarian paprika but Albert Szent Gyorgy. Agree?

26. "No man can discover his own talent." Brendan Francis.

I wonder who can do it if man himself cannot. That is man's own gift its own property given to him. Agree?

27. "A person has the right, and I think the responsibility, to develop all their talents.'

Jessye Norman

Not only to discover but also to develop through right educational program. While you work you grow and talent mature. Agree?

28. *"In the time one is given the steward must make the most of the talent one is given by the Lord."* Gloria Macapagal Arroyo

Talent is not only free gift but also great responsibility to use it for good intention. Agree?

29. *"True happiness involves the full use of one's power and talent."* John W. Gardner.

Talent as a skill always performs base upon its ability being supported with many different powers to accomplish its given goal. Talent on first place is given according to person's ability in order to fulfill its given duty. Agree?

30. *"Let start with recognizing your talents and finding ways to serve others by using them."*

Thomas Kinkale

Talent's purpose is to do good for others. Agree?

31. *"Let the beauty of what you love be what you do."* Yiddish proverbs.

As humans talent is power of love then talent's way is what you do and what you love.

32. *"I don't measure a man success by how high climbs but how high he bounces when he hits bottom."* George S. Patton.

Talent is our hope that will act in every difficult situation. Talent is master of our lives what makes a great difference between those that have it and those they do not.

33. *"Hide not your talents. They for use were made. What is a sundial in the shadow."*

Benjamin Franklin.

It is made to be use in every opportunity. They are our lives our life direction our opportunities.

34. *"Any human anywhere will blossom in a hundred unexpected talents and capacities simple by being given the opportunity to do so."* D. Lessing

That is all in the power of educated and productive society. Agree?

35. *"Our opportunities to do good are our talents."* Cotton Matter

Talent is our opportunity when ever opportunity opens its door. Talent never closes its eyes because it is all the time in action. Agree?

36. *"Set life's rhythm with your heart-drum."* Jonathan Lockwood Huie.

Keep your heart pace where talent is your drummer. One step at the time. Agree?

37. *"Don't let the noise of other's opinion drawn out your inner voice."* Steven Jobs

Listen to your heart it is your inner voice where your talent abides. Agree?

38. *"Say No to the demands of the world. Say YES to the longing of your own heart."*

Jonathan Lockwood Huie.

Follow your heart your talent your life direction. Agree?

39. *"Listen to the compass of your heart. All you need lies within you."* Mary Anne Radmacher.

Talent is the power of love in your heart your compass your life direction. Agree?

40. *"Everyone who wills can hear the inner voice. It is within everybody."* Gandhi

It is in your heart where your talent abides your life purpose. Agree?

41. "When I let go of what I am, I become what might be." Lao Tzu.

I am born to be something and I become someone what I might be according to my Talent.

Agree?

42. "He that would fish, must venture bait." Benjamin Franklin

If you like to be successful you must on first place venture talent. Agree?

43. "Faith is taking the first step, even when you don't see the whole staircase.." Martin Luther King, Jr.

Trust into your talent to take you into the land of darkness as lend of unknown. Discovery.

Agree.?

44. "The future belongs to those who believe in the beauty of their dreams." Eleanor Roosevelt.

Keep dreaming O' you Talented man and let your Talent do the work of your dreams. Agree?

45. "Look well into thyself, there is a source of strength which will always spring up if you will.

Always look there." Marcus Aurelius.

Talent supported by your will power create your inner strength. Agree?

46. "What is to give light must endure the burning." Eleanor Roosevelt

Talent brings light to this dark world only by enduring all necessary burning heath. Agree?

*47. "To live is to choose. But to choose well, you must know who you are and what you stand for, w*here you want to go and why you want to get there."
Kofi Annan

You are what your talent is and you go in its direction toward your purpose what your talent is."

Agree?

48. "Two roads diverge in a wood, and I look the one less traveled by, and that has made all the difference,: Robert Frost.

There are two ways of living. One is through well established, well known orthodox way where everything is the same day after day, and others one is the new way, way of new discovery as talents way where every talent goes. Agree?

49. "Choose your life purpose, and excel at living into that purpose." Jonathan Lockwood Huie

Talent is your life direction and your life purpose. Keep it. Agree?

50. *"Happiness lies in the joy of achievement and the thrill of creative effort,"* Franklin D. Roosevelt.

Every talent leads to the end of predictive program that on end always brings the joy and happiness. That we may say that talent is happiness. Agree?

51. *"Everything has beauty but not everyone sees it."* "Confucius

It is the talent that sees beauty and leads you toward it. That is the beauty that always brings happiness.

52. *"Once you make a decision the universe conspire to make it happen."* Ralph Waldo

Emerson.

When you act with you talent you are never ever alone. Agree?

53. *"We must believe that when we act with our talent we are never alone because talent is*

Universal, because every child is born with talent." Dragan.

Every child arrive to this world with talent in its heart and no one is rejected.

54. *"To leave the world a bit better... to know that one life has breathed easier because of you have lived. This is to have succeeded."* Ralph Waldo Emerson.

That is what talent is for. Keep it and your life will be blessed.

55. *"A ship in harbor is safe, but that is not what ships are for."* John A. Shedd

It is gift that is made for use. Use your talent and do good as a life purpose. Agree?

56. *"If a man does not know what port he is steering for, no wind is favorable to him."*

Seneca.

Talent is your life direction. Trust and follow it.

57. *"Have the courage to follow your heart and intuition-they somehow already know what you truly want to become."* Steve Jobs

You are born to be and to become what your talent is. Be brave and courageous for you will never be alone, your talent will be your life purpose for the rest of your life.

58. *"Life in creativity is power in everyone born to live, to discover and to innovate."* Dragan

That is the fate that everyone has its own already coming in this world.

59. *"Ability is what you are capable of doing. Talent determines how well you do it."* modify Leo Holtz.

Ability is your born power to do things, but you cannot do it without talent what brings skill to do with your born ability. One is power and other one is skill. One is born with ability and then

Talent is given accordingly. Agree?

60. *"All of us do not have equal talents, but all of us should have an equal opportunity to develop out talent."* John Fitzgerald Kennedy.

That should be what this book purpose is for opportunity to become privilege of all. Agree?

61. *"The boldness of endurance is the underline to almost every success."* Mary Anne

Radmacher.

Endurance is part of human's ability as one of supporter for human's talent. There are only two thing as Ability which is mainly endurance perseverance will power and many others inborn qualities as a foundation for given TALENT. Agree?

62. *"The future belongs to those who believe in the beauty of their dreams."* Eleanor Roosevelt

Only talent dreams real dream. Keep dreaming and let your talent do the work of your dreams.

Agree?

63. *"What lies behind us and what lies before us are tiny matters compared to what lies within us.*

"Ralph Waldo Emerson.

Talent abides as a power of love in our heart. Agree?

64. *"It takes courage to grow and become who you are."* e. e. Cummings.

It takes long hard end enduring way from moment you discover who you are born to be to the moment you become according to your talent and ready to start acting accordingly. Those are the years of persistence. Agree

65. *"If we don't change, we don't grow. If we don't grow, we aren't really living.""* Gail Sheehe

While you grow, your body grow your talent mature. On who grows also become old while talent never gets old but only mature. Agree?

66. *"All our dreams can come true, if we have the courage to pursue them."* Walt Disney.

Talent always dream real dreams and courage is one that opens that heavy door. Agree?.

67. *"What we have done for ourselves alone dies within us; what we have done for others and the world remains and is immortal."* Albert Pike

Difference between talented one and one without is immortality. Agree?.

68. *"The purpose of human life is to serve, and to show compassion and the will to help others."*

Albert Schweitzer.

Talent is our life purpose. Agree?

69. *"Whatever you can do, or dream you can. Begin it. Boldness has genius, power and magic in it. Begin it now.* Johan Wolfgang von Goethe.

Powerful talent dreams powerful dreams having power to make its dream reality. That is what we may call being bold. Agree?

70. *"Do not dwell in the past, do not dream of the future, concentrate the mind on the present time."* The Buddha.

When talent acts there is no past and there is no future, but only present time when power of work is in 101%. Concentration on work produce 101% result. Agree?

71. *"The purpose of our lives is to be happy."* Tenzin Gyatso. the 14 Dalai Lama

Talent is our life purpose our life happiness. Agree

72. *"If you are not in the moment, you are either looking forward to uncertainty, or back to pain and regret."* Jim Carrey

Talent is the your given power your skill that is only at present while acting. For talent when acts there is only and only the present time. There is no looking back or dreaming for future at that time. Agree?

73. *"If you don't know where you are going, any road will take you there."* Lewis Carroll.

Without talent there is no life direction and life goes to any road. Agree?

74. *"The goal of life is to make your heartbeat match the beat of the Universe, to match your nature with nature."* Joseph Campbell.

Talent in our heart is from universe to naturally keep rhythm of the universe as our nature with nature itself because "nature created us from the same sources and to the same end.

From dust to dust. Seneca. Agree?

75. *"The meaning of life is not simple to exist, to survive, but to move ahead, to go up, to achieve, to conquer."* Arnold Schwarzenegger

That what Talent is for, to move and o succeed. Agree?.

76. *"Unless you try to do something beyond what you have already mastered, you will never grow."* Ralph Waldo Emerson.

Humans grow with activities but talent mature with every new action. Agree?.

77. *"Destiny is not a matter of chance, it is matter of choice. It is not something to be waited for, but rather something to be attained."* William Jennings Bryan.

Your destiny is in your talent your gift to be mastered and to be utilized to the last atom of its power. Talent is like electricity like time lasting battery to be used completely. Agree?

78. *"Life is not easy for any of us. But what of that? We must have perseverance and above all confidence in ourselves. We must believe that we are gifted for something and that this thing must be attained."* Marie Curie.

Trust in your talent and persevere. Agree?

79. *"Success is not the key to happiness. Happiness is the key to success. If you love what you are doing, you will be successful. "*Albert Schweitzer

Talent is on first place love what you are doing and happiness always comes on the end of path.

Agree?

80 *"I make a living doing what I love doing, and it is what brings me joy."* Tom Cochrane

Talent is love and talent loves what one is doing. That is cardinal characteristic of every active talent. Agree#

81. *"Behind an able man, there are always other able man."* Chinese prov

However behind every talented successful man there is always loving mother. Agree?

About the Book

I never thought about human's talent prior I had opportunity to read about my Granddaughter introduction to Orthopedic Surgery at Washington University at St. Luis.

"I knew I wanted to be a physician since fifth grade. Dr. Lily Bogunovic. Rest is describe in Toto in my book.

Word talent has been used in human's conversation for centuries without any deep meaning as humans talent deserve as a essential part of humans life as for every humans life direction and life purpose to be realized in period depending on the power of given talent as every electrical power that we are not able to see but only to observe it given fruits-result.

What talent is no one can confirm with certainty because no one ever seen talent that is as I said like electrical power that we see not but what we see its light that is result of that invisible power.

There are many different believe about what talent is and is no argument on my side because I do respect everybody's opinion and believe with assumption that talent is everybody's personal property as I do call gift that is given free but not with free responsibilities that are much expensive.

Talent is as I intended to present as a power of love that is in the heart that must be born mainly in loving and carrying family where mother has essential importance together with fathers support.

Born in Family and later dressed or better to say educated in education as a best way for the future of that given gift.

Talent was dressed in education to be indoctrinated in society by providing adequate place for its activities.

We must accept that talent is like Duracell batteries with limited lasting that must be utilize in given time. I personally worked 50 years as medical doctor to finish in time when I felt that here is no more power in my battery-my talent and that I am at present time alone in this world ready to retire.

My goal is to share my experience with my children that are born with different talent to become and to enter our society ready for their life duty according to given talents. D.P. B.

Printed in the United States
By Bookmasters